INTERNATIONAL DEVELOPMENT IN FOCUS

Playing to Strengths
A Policy Framework for Mainstreaming Northeast India

SANJAY KATHURIA AND PRIYA MATHUR, EDITORS

Contents

Boxes

Figures

Tables

Note: The findings of this study are not binding on the countries covered by the study.

Foreword

The North Eastern Region (NER), with its human capital, abundant natural resources, favorable climate, and diverse agroclimatic zones, has significant economic growth potential.

India's Act East policy, and its aim to strengthen economic prosperity in NER, offers the opportunity to unlock the region's comparative advantage. Increased engagement between India and Bangladesh and among Bangladesh, Bhutan, India, and Nepal can strengthen connectivity and lower transportation costs between NER and the rest of India and neighboring countries.

Improved connectivity can yield easier access to inputs and markets, allowing value chains to scale up. The price of goods and services can be held in check with lower transport costs, enhancing consumer welfare and reducing poverty. Improvements in regional connectivity open up Bangladesh to economic opportunities for investment in NER, and create new markets for NER products in Bangladesh that benefit firms and households.

This report can be commended on many grounds. It provides guidance on policies to unleash the economic potential of NER and leverage growth opportunities. Together with a companion volume, "Strengthening Cross-Border Value Chains: Opportunities for India and Bangladesh," it will encourage informed policy debate and provide policymakers in India and Bangladesh with a foundation to enable shared prosperity.

Junaid Ahmad
Country Director, India

Zoubida Kherous Allaoua
Regional Director
Equitable Growth, Finance and Institutions
South Asia

Acknowledgments

This report was prepared as part of a larger study on strengthening cross-border value chains in Northeast India, which was carried out by a core team led by Sanjay Kathuria and Priya Mathur and which included Emiliano Duch, Prabir De, Charles Kunaka, Michael Friis Jensen, Thirumalai G. Srinivasan, Ciliaka Millicent W. Gitau, Ruchita Manghnani, Aman Khanna, and Nadeem Rizwan. Special thanks to Emiliano Duch, Maria Deborah Kim, and Gloria Ferrer Morera for mentoring and guiding the value chain studies. Grace James, Savita Dhingra, Rima Sukhija, and (earlier) Shiny Jaison supported the team during the entire cycle of production. The primary authors of each chapter in this report were as follows: chapter 1, Sanjay Kathuria and Priya Mathur; chapter 2, Thirumalai G. Srinivasan; chapter 3, Prabir De and Charles Kunaka; and chapter 4, Michael Friis Jensen.

The team thanks the following for very helpful comments and reviews: Chakib Jenane, Anupam Joshi, Tesfamichael Nahusenay, Soujanya Krishna Chodavarapu, and Janardan Prasad Singh. The team also benefited from interaction with Priti Kumar, Varun Singh, and Manivannan Pathy throughout the life of the project.

The report was prepared under the guidance of Manuela Francisco and (earlier) Esperanza Lasagabaster, and under the stewardship of Junaid Ahmad and Robert Saum. Editing was done by Sharanya Ramesh and Sandra Gain.

The team would like to place on record its sincere appreciation to the Department of Foreign Affairs and Trade, Government of Australia, for its steadfast support for the preparation of the report and the overall regional trade agenda in South Asia. The team is also grateful to the Ministry for Development of the North Eastern Region, Government of India, as well as the state governments of the Northeast Indian states for their cooperation. The team would also like to thank the Federation of Indian Chambers of Commerce and Industry and the Indian Chamber of Commerce for extending their support in connecting the team to private sector players and other stakeholders in the North Eastern Region during field work for this study.

About the Contributors

EDITORS

Sanjay Kathuria is Lead Economist and Coordinator, South Asia Regional Integration, in the World Bank's Macroeconomics, Trade, and Investment Global Practice, based in Washington, DC. During his more than 27 years at the World Bank, he has worked in several regions, including Europe and Central Asia, Latin America and the Caribbean, and South Asia. Prior to joining the World Bank, he was a Fellow at the Indian Council for Research on International Economic Relations in New Delhi. He graduated from St. Stephen's College, and he received his master's degree from the Delhi School of Economics and his doctorate from Oxford University. His research interests include economic growth, international trade and trade policy, economic integration, competitiveness, technology development, fiscal policy, and financial sector development.

Priya Mathur has been working in development as an economist. Currently, she works with the World Bank on international trade and regional integration, global value chains, and entrepreneurship. She has also worked in the private sector as a strategy consultant with the Boston Consulting Group. In that role, she has worked with firms in telecommunications and in banking and asset management. She has an M.Phil and a master's degree in economics from the Delhi School of Economics in Delhi; she graduated from the Post Graduate Program in Management at the Indian School of Business in Hyderabad.

AUTHORS

Prabir De is a Professor and Head of the ASEAN-India Centre (AIC) at Research and Information System for Developing Countries (RIS), New Delhi. He works in the field of international economics, with a focus on trade facilitation and connectivity.

Michael Friis Jensen is a Consultant and Agricultural Economist who works to smooth trade through the lowering of nontariff barriers and the modernization of quality infrastructure.

Charles Kunaka is a Lead Private Sector Specialist with the Trade and Regional Integration Unit of the World Bank. He works on trade and transport connectivity, logistics, and trade corridor development projects.

Thirumalai G. Srinivasan is a Consultant Economist. His current research focus is on development macroeconomics, international trade, and poverty with a spatial perspective. His previous work at the World Bank centered on developing countries in the South Asia and Middle East and North Africa regions.

Abbreviations

ADB	Asian Development Bank
ADBI	Asian Development Bank Institute
AIC-RIS	ASEAN-India Centre at RIS
ASEAN	Association of Southeast Asian Nations
BBIN	Bangladesh-Bhutan-India-Nepal
BCIM-EC	Bangladesh-China-India-Myanmar Economic Corridor
BFSA	Bangladesh Food Safety Authority
BG	broad gauge
BIS	Bureau of Indian Standards
BSTI	Bangladesh Standards and Testing Institution
CUTS	Consumer Utility and Trust Society
DFID	Department for International Development (United Kingdom)
DGCIS	Directorate General of Commercial Intelligence Statistics
EIC	Export Inspection Council
FAO	Food and Agriculture Organization of the United Nations
FICCI	Federation of Indian Chambers of Commerce and Industry
FSSAI	Food Safety and Standards Authority of India
GAP	Good Agricultural Practices
GCA	gross cropped area
GDP	gross domestic product
GIS	geographic information system
GSDP	gross state domestic product
GST	goods and services tax
GSVA	gross state value added
ILRI	International Livestock Research Institute
ILS	Instrument Landing Systems
IWAI	Inland Waterways Authority of India
IWT	inland waterways transport
JICA	Japan International Cooperation Agency
km	kilometers
LCS	land customs station
MDoNER	Ministry of Development of the North Eastern Region
MORTH	Ministry of Road Transport and Highways

MVA	Motor Vehicles Agreement
NABL	National Accreditation Board for Testing and Calibration Laboratories
NEIIPP	North East Industrial and Investment Promotion Policy
NER	North Eastern Region
NSSO	National Sample Survey Office
NTM	nontariff measure
NW-2	National Waterway 2
OECD	Organisation for Economic Co-operation and Development
PIWTT	Protocol on Inland Water Transit and Trade
RCA	revealed comparative advantage
RITES	Rail India Technical and Economic Service
RIS	Research and Information System for Developing Countries
SAR	special administrative region
SARDP-NE	Special Accelerated Road Development Programme for the North Eastern Region
SITC	Standard International Trade Classification
SPS	sanitary and phytosanitary standards
TBT	technical barrier to trade
tkm	tonne-kilometer
UNICEF	United Nations Children's Fund
USDA	United States Department of Agriculture
WHO	World Health Organization
WTO	World Trade Organization
WUR	Wageningen University & Research

All monetary amounts are U.S. dollars unless otherwise indicated.

1 A Policy Framework to Build on Northeast India's Strengths

SANJAY KATHURIA AND PRIYA MATHUR

FAVORABLE DYNAMICS

What does the North Eastern Region (NER)[1] of India remind one of? To the first-time traveler, a beautiful climate, a high percentage of women working, clean air, low population density, and expertise in English may stand out. This is consistent with the more data-driven picture of NER—a region with advantages of climate, topography, and human resources—in turn reflected in the potential of its agriculture and service sectors.

However, post-1947 history created conditions that stifled NER's development. Seven decades ago, NER's cord between India and the world was cut, and it became geographically isolated, connected to the rest of India only through the narrow Siliguri Corridor, or "Chicken's Neck." Once in the forefront of India's development (Government of India 2008), NER gradually began to lag other regions, including other comparable hill states in India—a stark reminder that distance and geography still matter for development, despite the rapid improvement in communications technology. The importance of distance is seen in the higher prices faced by consumers in the states of NER. Compared with West Bengal, the nearest Indian state with a seaport, the poor in NER face 60 percent higher prices in rural areas and 30 percent higher prices in urban areas.

This picture of NER's isolation is now changing. Over the past decade, connectivity agreements with Bangladesh and accelerating infrastructure investments in NER and its neighbors have begun to reduce the subregion's economic isolation. In every state in NER, the average time to reach the nearest city has been cut from more than three hours in 2000 to one hour in 2015. These developments in connectivity are akin to a reduction in taxes on exports and imports, and they ultimately bring to the consumer the benefits of lower prices and a greater variety of products.

Other global trends are also very favorable for NER. These include growing incomes, leisure spending, and consumer awareness in India and neighboring countries; a rising preference for fresh, healthful, safe, environmentally friendly, and socially responsible products; and the growing role of services in manufacturing, which is increasing demand for skilled resources.

Together, these developments can help NER showcase its strengths in agriculture and services. In fruits and spices, NER has an above-average share of cropped area, higher than that for all-India. NER's female adult literacy and female labor force participation rates are much higher than those for all-India. And in NER, the share of the tertiary sector in gross state domestic product (GSDP) has been at or above the median for all states in India. In addition, many of the crops are grown in organic or near-organic conditions; the air is fresh; and nature is bountiful.

To give a few specific examples, NER can capitalize on rising demand for fresh fruits and vegetables, and for fresh, high-quality spices. It can promote bamboo, an environmentally friendly resource. It can push nature-based tourism, as well as trade in medical and education services. These examples are not exhaustive, but they represent some of the immediate possibilities for the region.

APPROACH OF THE ANALYSIS

To explore how these developments have affected NER's competitiveness, the World Bank, in consultation with stakeholders—government, private sector, and academia—decided on a two-pronged approach. At the policy level, two cross-cutting constraints that are encountered across all sectors in NER were identified for deeper analysis: connectivity and logistics, and product standards and quality infrastructure. To ground the policy in specific contexts, the team studied four sectors in depth—fruits and vegetables, spices, bamboo and related products, and medical tourism. These sectors are illustrative and not meant to pick winners (annex 1A). Within the identified sectors, the team focused on "high-impact" segments that capitalize on changing consumer preferences to allow higher potential returns to women and those in the bottom 40 percent of the segment.

To cover the diverse states in NER but maintain the study's focus, the team concentrated on three states: Mizoram, which shares a border with Bangladesh and Myanmar; Tripura, for its geographic proximity and cultural affinity with Bangladesh and the presence of NER's only Integrated Check Post; and Assam, which is the junction of all the logistics networks in NER. However, the study findings should be applicable across states.

This study is unique in various ways. First, it combines the larger picture of NER, focusing on its strengths against the backdrop of global trends, with a detailed analysis of selected sectors to identify how value chains that leverage the strengths of NER can be scaled up. Second, it brings the demand side into focus, considering how changing consumer preferences affect the nature of global demand, and emphasizes the need to reorient the supply base in NER toward serving this changing demand. Third, it applies an explicit lens to the analysis of the value chain that focuses on women and the bottom 40 percent of the workforce pyramid. In NER, existing product value chains serve market segments in which most of the margin is appropriated by others, for example, intermediaries and processors in fruits and vegetables and spices, and doctors and hospitals in medical services. This study tries to identify product-market combinations (strategic segments) or value chains within a sector[2] that can create more and better job opportunities for women and the poor (referred to as high-impact value chains). Fourth, the approach highlights the role that technology can play in realizing the potential of high-impact value chains in sectors in which NER has an inherent advantage.

This report contains four chapters. Chapter 2 presents an overview of NER, drawing out its strengths and how they can be leveraged to participate in the global economy. Chapters 3 and 4, respectively, focus on the two cross-cutting constraints—connectivity and logistics, and product standards and related procedures. Chapter 1 draws on chapters 2 to 4, as well as on the in-depth analysis of the four sectors, which identifies high-impact value chains in each sector (see annex 1A) and suggests how they can be strengthened (Khanna 2019; Gitau 2019; Manghnani 2019; Mathur 2019).

TOWARD A POLICY FRAMEWORK

This report provides an initial policy framework that, by combining the supply and demand sides, adds a new dimension to current policy thinking on NER. It focuses on NER's strengths in the context of global trends. NER's key advantages lie in the agriculture and service sectors. The region has a strong comparative advantage in a variety of horticultural crops (fruits, spices) that are organic or near-organic. It also has a youthful, highly educated workforce, with high female labor force participation and proficiency in English, and a strong service sector orientation. NER can use these attributes to take advantage of global trends—growing consumer incomes, purchasing power, and awareness in India and abroad, which are driving the demand for fresh, healthful, safe, environmentally friendly, and socially responsible products—and the growing role of services in manufacturing, which is driving the demand for skilled human resources.

This policy chapter focuses on the following areas:

- Optimizing the developments in connectivity, focusing on synergies between different modes of transport, across investments between NER and neighboring states and countries, and softer investments in trade facilitation
- Leveraging the private sector to maximize the impact of quality infrastructure and focusing on clear demand for quality services
- Creating a "Brand North East" that focuses on several attributes that, taken together, constitute a unique value proposition

MAXIMIZING THE IMPACT OF CONNECTIVITY INVESTMENTS

The transport and logistics networks of NER and the surrounding area are evolving rapidly. Major developments include the extensions of the national highway network and three newly emerging corridors with neighboring countries: the Trilateral Highway linking India with Myanmar and Thailand; the Kaladan multimodal corridor linking the Port of Sittwe in Myanmar to NER states; and the Bangladesh-China-India-Myanmar economic corridor. Another major development is the extension of the broad-gauge railway network, which aims to connect all the state capitals in NER; construction is also under way toward the border with plans eventually to connect with Bangladesh and further to Kolkata. In addition, there are plans to improve navigation of the

Brahmaputra River (National Waterway 2), which will restore efficient use of what will be a low-cost transport option. The government has also announced plans to make more airports operational in NER and enhance direct air connectivity between Guwahati (Assam), the regional hub, and key destinations in South Asia and Southeast Asia. Trade facilitation efforts are also under way. Regionally, this is being done through measures such as the Bangladesh-Bhutan-India-Nepal (BBIN), Motor Vehicles Agreement (MVA), which when implemented will allow vehicles to cross borders in the region without the need for transloading cargo or passengers; bilateral measures include recognition in April 2017 by the Food Safety and Standards Authority of India of testing and certification by the Bangladesh Standards and Testing Institution for imports of 21 Bangladeshi food products into India.[3]

Enhancing NER's connectivity will require investment as well as policy reforms. Although the national government as well as NER states will need to undertake specific reforms, involving the private sector as a direct beneficiary will help maximize impact. Private sector participation will also be needed for investments in the provision of logistics services such as aggregation and collection, as well as the cold chains required by high-impact fresh value chains in horticulture and animal products. The priority reforms are outlined in the following subsections.

Developing logistics hubs and corridors

NER is characterized by thin populations dispersed over difficult terrain. To leverage the investments in highways and railways, it will be necessary to consolidate traffic along a few long-distance corridors and at a few nodes. The same principles would apply to air transport. Based on the intersections of the traditional and emerging new trade routes, three locations could be developed as logistics hubs for NER: Guwahati (Assam), Agartala (Tripura), and Silchar (Assam).

To develop these locations into viable and beneficial clusters, it is important to analyze the likely trade flows and functions that each cluster can perform; develop first- and last-mile connectivity links and facilities; engage with the private sector, which will be required to invest in the services and supply chains to be served; make land available at the right locations; and consider other incentives that may be offered to the investors in each potential cluster. One of the critical services that will be required is that for cold chains, to support the fresh produce the region produces and of which it could produce more.

Plugging the gaps in transport networks: Ensuring interoperability of transport systems

The government of India is investing heavily in new road, rail, air, water, and border infrastructure. It is important that the countries of the region standardize their infrastructure standards, especially along the major corridors, to allow seamless cross-border services. Currently, for instance, there are differences in vehicle axle load limits between India, Bangladesh, Myanmar, and Thailand. Similarly, railways in the region have a combination of meter and broad-gauge lines. The BBIN MVA provides one of the building blocks for uninterrupted traffic flows within the South Asia region. However, in addition to such agreements, it is important for the countries to negotiate complementary reforms in, for instance, road signage, driver training, and insurance.

Improving trade facilitation

The challenges with trade facilitation between NER and neighboring countries are most visible at the land border crossing points. Goods must be transloaded between vehicles of different countries, and the clearance processes are lengthy, which adds to the time and cost of transportation. Seamless movement of traffic across borders will require efforts along several dimensions, such as allowing cargo vehicles to cross borders; creating adequate space for transloading until such a system prevails; aligning and widening access roads and creating adequate space for parking on both sides of the border crossing point; allowing processing of split consignments; introducing a system of prearrival processing of documents; and synchronizing border opening hours on the two sides. Training is necessary for border officials and private sector users (customs brokers, transporters, traders, and laborers) on the current trade policy between the two countries and associated processes, as a recent World Bank report highlights (Kathuria 2018).

Modernizing private sector logistics practices

The private sector could be encouraged to invest in handling facilities and warehouses. One of the major sources of inefficiency at the border posts is the use of manual labor to transload cargo from the trucks of one country to those of another. This process could be made more efficient, especially for the major shippers, by adopting the use of pallets[4] and deploying mechanized means for the transfer, such as forklift trucks. In Southeast Asia, it takes only a few minutes to transload cargo through the use of containers and provision of appropriate cranes at the border posts. Some of the cranes are privately owned, and a fee is payable for the transloading operation.

Overall, the logistics services markets in NER could also be opened to Bangladeshi operators and vice versa, especially once the railway connectivity to the Port of Chittagong is completed. This will facilitate the smooth clearance and movement of containers from the port to and from destinations across NER. This provides one example of win-win opportunities for NER and Bangladesh in cross-border value chains in the region (box 1.1).

Introducing a through-transit system

The absence of integrated and modern transit systems has long been an impediment to transit traffic across South Asia. The current practice of transloading cargo from the trucks of one country to the trucks of the other country at border points, except between India and Nepal, is inefficient. The same applies to railways, where locomotives must be changed. The recently adopted BBIN MVA provides a framework (not yet operational) for Indian traffic to cross from the rest of India to the NER states across Bangladesh, which would drastically reduce the travel distance.

A functional through-transit system between the countries of South Asia and between South Asia and the countries of the Association of Southeast Asian Nations (ASEAN) has the potential to transform the trade facilitation

BOX 1.1

Cross-border value chains create win-win opportunities for NER and Bangladesh

Bangladesh can play an important role in the development of high-impact value chains, which will also bring gains to consumers and firms in Bangladesh.

First, Bangladesh can serve as a key proximate market for products from India's North Eastern Region (NER), and consumers in Bangladesh can gain through access to a greater variety of goods and services. For instance, fresh horticultural products from NER can help meet Bangladesh's food requirements, including fruits, vegetables, and spices (table B1.1.1). Already, various horticultural products from NER reach Bangladesh, with informal exports far exceeding formal exports.[a] In services such as medical tourism, Bangladesh could be an important market for NER, given Bangladesh's current position as the largest source of medical tourists to India, and its geographic and cultural proximity to NER. Bangladesh contributed 35 percent of India's estimated medical tourists and 55 percent of India's estimated medical tourism revenues in 2015–16.[b]

Second, Bangladeshi firms can help NER value chains and businesses scale up, while availing themselves of growth opportunities. They would benefit from access to a greater variety of possibly cheaper inputs, as well as access to NER markets (and beyond, with transit through NER) for finished products. For example, horticultural produce from NER could provide inputs for Bangladesh's vibrant food-processing industry, while processed foods could be exported to NER and beyond; this is already taking place. Land is relatively scarce in Bangladesh; Bangladeshi firms could secure a steady supply of inputs to meet the food requirements of a growing population by investing in NER's farm sector. They could similarly invest in processing plants in NER, sourcing some inputs locally, and then sell in NER as well as reexport to Bangladesh—PRAN foods of Bangladesh has already set up a plant in Tripura. Investment in NER can also serve as a learning ground for Bangladeshi firms. For instance, in the medical tourism value chain, Bangladeshi hospitals can participate in the initial diagnostics before a patient travels abroad for a medical procedure, as well as the aftercare when a patient returns home. Joint ventures with destination hospitals in NER would facilitate the knowledge transfer that would enable hospitals in Bangladesh to perform additional medical procedures.

Third, Bangladesh and NER can both gain from improved scope and efficiency of logistics and logistics service firms. Movement through Bangladesh and use of Bangladeshi ports can improve NER's access to markets, reducing transportation costs and time, and making NER products more competitive. At the same time, NER value chains can create business opportunities for Bangladeshi logistics providers. Further, reciprocal transit arrangements through India, especially NER, and the use of emerging corridors with neighboring countries can allow Bangladeshi firms easier access to markets for sourcing inputs or selling products in Bangladesh, Bhutan, India, Myanmar, Nepal, and beyond. For greater efficiency gains, governments could consider opening the logistics services market in NER to Bangladeshi operators and vice versa.

TABLE B1.1.1 **Bangladesh's food trade, 2015**

$, millions

	FRUITS AND VEGETABLES (1)	SPICES (2)	ALL FOOD ITEMS (3)
Imports	991.9	215.7	6,870.9
Exports	168.7	24.2	789.0
Net food imports	823.1	191.5	6,081.9

Sources: Calculations based on data from the United Nations Commodity Trade Statistics Database, United Nations, New York (accessed March 11, 2019), http://comtrade.un.org/db/; and World Integrated Trade Solution (database), World Bank, Washington, DC (accessed March 11, 2019), http://wits.worldbank.org/WITS/.
Note: Under Standard International Trade Classification (SITC) Rev. 3: (1) SITC 05: Vegetables and fruit; (2) SITC 075: Spices; (3) all food items include SITC 0: Food and live animals (excluding SITC 00: Live animals and SITC 08: Feedstuff for animals), SITC 111: Non-alcoholic beverages, n.e.s.; and SITC 4: Animal and vegetable oils, fats, and waxes. N.e.s. = not elsewhere specified.

Sources: Nath (2012); Government of India (2017b).
a. Nath (2012) provides estimates of formal and informal trade between the state of Tripura in NER and Bangladesh based on a survey carried out in September–December 2011 and February 2012.
b. Government of India (2017b). The report estimates 460,000 medical tourists and $620 million in tourism revenue in India.

environment in the region, especially for the landlocked countries. A practical transit solution on a few identified road corridors with significant traffic potential is required. Some of the road traffic currently moving through the Chicken's Neck in particular could move through Bangladesh, with significant savings in shipping times and costs, if a functional transit procedure through Bangladesh were in place. Such a transit system would (1) allow seamless movement of goods between West Bengal and NER, with no significant waiting time at the border or en route due to inspections or transloading; and (2) incorporate adequate cost recovery mechanisms to enable Bangladesh to recoup the costs associated with the required infrastructure and services, according to universal principles on freedom of transit.

Tapping the potential of low-cost inland waterways

There are challenges to effectively utilizing the waterways in the region. These include heavy siltation, shifting channels, lack of adequate depth of water during the lean season, constraints on night navigation, and the absence of other navigation aids in many parts of the channels in the Brahmaputra and Barak Rivers. Links to other forms of connectivity, such as roads and railways, as well as digital connectivity (mobile, phone, and Internet), can help increase the benefits of the waterways in the region.

Recent developments—such as the signing in 2017 of a memorandum of understanding between Bangladesh and Bhutan on the use of inland waterways for bilateral trade and transit cargo, as well as on passenger and cruise services on the coastal and protocol routes between India and Bangladesh—make it evident that inland navigation is gaining greater traction in the Bay of Bengal subregion.

Therefore, developing an integrated transport plan with special emphasis on multimodal connectivity would open this isolated region to its neighbors and the rest of the world.

Expanding air connectivity

NER is well suited for the production of fresh produce, especially vegetables, fruits, and flowers. It is rich in natural and cultural assets, which makes it an attractive destination for tourists. Given NER's relative strengths in services, it can also develop into a viable destination for those seeking education and medical services. Given its difficult terrain and distance from markets in the rest of India, air transport has significant potential to sustain commerce and tourism and realize the potential of horticulture in the region. A proposal to develop more airports is quite appropriate. However, it will need to be accompanied by careful route planning and scheduling to consolidate shipments to ensure commercial viability, while also maintaining regular schedules to key markets to retain market share. For network expansion, the proposed direct connectivity with neighbors such as Bangladesh, Myanmar, Nepal, and Thailand should have a significant impact on NER. Exploiting the full potential of regional air connectivity will require supportive policy reforms, especially with respect to visa requirements. This is particularly the case with Bangladesh, which is a main source of medical tourists to India and could be the largest potential source for medical tourists to NER, but Bangladesh is not part of the e-visa procedures that India has in place for most other countries.

ADOPTING A DEMAND-BASED APPROACH TO PRODUCT STANDARDS

In NER, production and trading structures are primarily traditional, dominated by small units and atomistic value chains exercising little vertical coordination. These structures are not conducive to upgrading quality. The demand for safer and higher-quality products is currently restrained by low incomes and poor connectivity to international markets. Niche products for discerning consumers are developing, although their volumes remain very small.

The region is waking up to improved connectivity as well as greater trading opportunities. Such opportunities are likely to be accompanied by increased pressure on producers from consumers, buyers, and regulators to upgrade the safety and quality of their products. First, the growth of income and awareness creates a growing segment of discerning consumers who are demanding high-quality products. Second, growing access to regional markets will grant NER's producers access to global value chains, which tend to use more stringent quality standards to coordinate their trade and satisfy distant customers. Third, regulators in India and other countries in the region are moving toward upgrading food safety and control by tightening legislation and improving the currently often lax and unsystematic enforcement. In this context, the following subsections propose ways to address challenges related to product standards and quality infrastructure.

Production and trading practices

Value chain interventions, especially in horticultural value chains, are critical for upgrading product quality in NER. NER's products often suffer from quality problems that will be solved not by focusing on investments in standards and related procedures but by improving production and trading practices. The development of services such as standards, testing, and certification would have the greatest chances of success if they were integrated into broader value chain development projects that also address production and trading practices. The latter are critical to producing a high-quality product and maintaining its quality until it reaches the consumer (see annex 1B).

Clearly identified demand for investments in quality infrastructure

Investments in quality infrastructure should focus on clearly identified demand from regulators or the business community. In addressing such demand, the government should leverage private sector services as much as possible. Further, government agencies should coordinate their plans to develop food laboratories, preferably by establishing a multiagency laboratory that could cater to several agencies, including border control. Several government authorities are already in the process of developing new food laboratories, such as in Assam and Tripura. The proliferation of laboratories and duplication of testing capacity in a region with evolving demand can undermine the sustainability of the investments. To support countries in drawing up a laboratory investment plan, the World Bank has developed a guide on how to invest in food laboratories (World Bank 2009).

Emerging products for discerning consumers

In developing standards and investing in testing services, attention could be given to emerging niche market products for discerning consumers—products such as organic foods or bamboo wood for construction. These products may need appropriate standards. In the case of bamboo, for example, the Indian government could influence the development of international grading standards to ensure that such standards capture the quality characteristics of bamboo from NER and other parts of the country.

Private food standards increasingly influence competitiveness and market access; Indian market participants also develop private standards. Such private initiatives often complement the efforts of government regulatory agencies. These agencies will likely include private initiatives directly in future regulation. The government may wish to influence the process of setting private standards, which are key to accessing global supply chains, and support their implementation.

The development of laboratories should also focus on such emerging products. During fieldwork in Assam, several private firms expressed demand for food testing for commercial purposes, mainly targeting the Indian market. However, some of these firms were skeptical that government laboratories would be able to develop a business culture suitable for commercial testing.

Cross-border trade through equivalence and mutual recognition agreements

International best practice suggests the use of trade facilitation tools—such as harmonization, equivalence, and mutual recognition—for import control. The authorities should rely as little as possible on the traditional model of 100 percent inspection and testing of imports. Investment in laboratories at the border posts should be kept low. Indeed, India, represented by the Food Safety and Standards Authority of India (FSSAI), is currently experimenting with the introduction of practices such as equivalence and mutual recognition. Recently, India demonstrated a willingness to recognize testing services in Bangladesh for exports of several processed food products from Bangladesh to India.

CREATING AND LEVERAGING "BRAND NORTH EAST"

NER could consider launching a "Brand North East" that emphasizes elements such as healthy living, environmental sustainability, social responsibility, and service orientation. These elements stem from NER's strengths: agroclimatic diversity reflected in the environment-friendly production of a varied basket of horticultural products; high female labor force participation rates that can feed into a narrative of socially responsible production; clean air, rich biodiversity, and unique cultural assets; and service orientation, as reflected in, for example, the large presence of NER natives in the hospitality and nursing sectors in India and widespread acknowledgment of their soft skills. These strengths add up to a set of distinct and unique characteristics. It is important to build a general brand that plays up these characteristics because, for the most part, NER products cannot compete on price with products from better-located or larger economic regions.

Although the global branding exercise could be leveraged for promotion of individual products from NER, the cluster promotion activities for specific sectors and value chains could in turn help strengthen the global brand. Promoting "inclusive" value chains, for instance, would reinforce Brand North East and its emphasis on social responsibility.

The creation of Brand North East will require coordination across state governments, which will be best carried out by regional coordinating agencies, such as the Ministry of Development of North Eastern Region (MDoNER) or the North East Council. It will also require coordination across government departments as well as with the private sector within individual states, especially for leveraging the brand for the promotion of specific products or clusters. For instance, promotion of the bamboo-related cluster, which is based on bamboo products with strict technical specifications targeting the eco-conscious consumer, may require coordination between the Departments of Agriculture, Forestry, and Commerce and Industries, as well as between the government and the private sector within a particular state and perhaps across states. Similarly, promotion of a medical tourism cluster that is based on providing long-duration complex services (such as cancer care, neurological treatment, fertility treatment, or organ transplants) may require coordination between the Departments of Health and Tourism, and between government and private sector entities such as hospitals, hotels, and travel agencies.

CONCLUSION

This report lays out an initial policy framework for NER that integrates the demand and supply sides and shows that even with a low base in manufacturing, NER can leverage its strengths in agriculture and services to step up its growth. In doing so, the report hopes to add a new dimension to policy discussions on NER, which have been somewhat ambivalent about the role of manufacturing in NER's development. However, implementing this framework will require a different approach to doing business compared, for example, with the ecosystem associated with the traditional value chains that currently exist in NER, which are geared mostly to local or price conscious consumers. New value chains could be started as pilot projects in a selected district or districts and expand their reach over time. The traditional value chains will, of course, continue to exist. The success of the new value chains will demonstrate their benefits, especially for women and the poor, and motivate more private sector players to try to emulate that success. The strengthening of such value chains will reduce migration and eventually bring requisite skills back to NER. This could help accelerate the transformation of NER into a mainstream participant and not just a cog, albeit a vital one, in the government of India's Act East policy.

ANNEX 1A: HIGH-IMPACT VALUE CHAINS IN SELECTED SECTORS IN THE NORTH EASTERN REGION OF INDIA

To illustrate the approach of this study, four sectors were identified, among the many promising sectors in NER, for in-depth value chain analysis: fruits and vegetables, spices, bamboo and related products, and medical tourism.

The choice of sectors was informed by stakeholder consultations and two key criteria—the sector's potential to generate more and better job opportunities, particularly for women and the bottom 40 percent of the workforce; and its potential to leverage cross-border opportunities provided by the deepening cooperation with Bangladesh. The first criterion was applied twice—first, to identify sectors for in-depth analysis, and then again, to identify a high-impact strategic segment within those sectors.

Every industry has several strategic segments. Each strategic segment is a function of the product variation and the user group served and has a unique value chain. Among the various strategic segments within each sector, the study identifies a high-impact strategic segment or value chain that could create better job opportunities and greater appropriable margins for women and the poor. The high-impact value chains thus identified are (1) fresh fruits and vegetables for quality-conscious consumers in the fruits and vegetables sector (Khanna 2019); (2) fresh spices for quality-conscious consumers in the spice sector (Gitau 2019); (3) bamboo products with strict technical specifications for eco-conscious consumers in the bamboo sector (Manghnani 2019); and (4) long-duration complex services (such as cancer treatment) clustered in Guwahati (Assam) as the hub, with other cities in NER and neighboring countries acting as spokes, in medical tourism (Mathur 2019).

For horticultural products such as fruits, vegetables, and spices, existing value chains in NER largely cater to the strategic segment comprising fresh products for price-conscious consumers and, to some extent, the segment comprising processed products for price-conscious consumers. Both are relatively low-margin segments and, even more significantly, bring very low returns to farmers and agricultural labor; most of the margins are appropriated by intermediate buyers, processors, and retailers.

In horticulture, fresh products catering to quality-conscious consumers have the highest return potential, as this strategic segment has the least competition, while discerning consumers are able and willing to pay more for high-quality products. The longer shelf life of processed products makes them more commoditized and tradable, allowing producers from around the world to compete in such products. Fresh products, with shorter shelf life, require frequent replenishment and delivery, and thus competition is limited to other producers that, through superior logistics, can deliver them quickly, frequently, and with their freshness intact. Fresh products catering to quality-conscious consumers face even less competition, given the smaller production base for high-quality products that meet the quality and quality assurance requirements (such as certification and traceability) of discerning consumers.

At the same time, fresh, high-quality products targeted at discerning customers have the potential to garner higher returns for farmers and agricultural labor, including women. Farmers and farmworkers create more value in this segment through use of the required better cultivation and harvest practices. They can potentially also appropriate higher margins because the smaller production base and quality and quality assurance requirements of consumers impart to them more bargaining power. The farmers' margins in this segment depend on how the rest of the value chain is organized—for instance, whether farmers sell to retailers or final customers directly or through an intermediary such as an export firm. (See annex 1B for an example of how blockchain technology is being used in horticultural value chains in Haiti to empower small farmers.) All activities along this value chain require more highly skilled labor to produce and preserve quality all the way to the consumer, which not only creates more jobs but has the potential to create better-paid ones. Because the participation of women already tends to be high in several activities in this value chain—such as the on-farm activities of cultivation and harvesting, sorting, grading, and packaging—this segment also creates more and better opportunities for women. There are also potential opportunities for women's participation in other activities that are more important in this value chain compared to other value chains (for example, research and development, quality assurance, and marketing and distribution), as workers or even, for example, as entrepreneurs in marketing and distribution firms.

NER is very rich in bamboo stock and diversity, but the industrial base of the bamboo cluster in the region is small. NER firms operate largely in the segment comprising simple traditional products that cater to consumers who are not necessarily interested in the ecofriendly characteristics of bamboo. Examples of these products include incense sticks, handicrafts, poles for agriculture and basic construction, mats, baskets, and pulp. The margins are low for enterprises in this segment; returns to farmers and laborers are also low.

The high-impact value chain in bamboo is the segment comprising bamboo products with hard technical specifications for eco-conscious consumers. Examples of such products include bamboo wood, high-end furniture, bamboo plywood, flooring and panels made of bamboo, home products with consistent quality and design, bamboo as an input for the production of clean biofuels like ethanol, bamboo fiber and textiles, bamboo to make car interiors, and bamboo as a material for 3D printing. Eco-conscious consumers care about the environment and are willing to pay a premium for products that are produced and sourced in a sustainable manner. Such consumers often reside in urban areas and advanced countries in Europe. The region should aspire to move in the medium-to-long term toward this segment. It is the most attractive segment, given the growth in demand globally and the rapidly evolving technology on the supply side. The margins are higher because eco-conscious consumers are willing to pay a premium for ecofriendly products, and high barriers to entry reduce competition compared to that in other segments. Further, the segment has the potential to provide relatively greater returns to the poor and women, compared with the other segments in the bamboo industry. The larger scale of operations, greater labor specialization requirements, and higher skill content compared with the other segments, as well as the traceability needs of consumers in this segment, ensure that the participants across the value chain and the workforce create more value and have the potential to appropriate higher margins. The segment has the potential for greater employment of women and the rural poor in the plantation sector and preprocessing sector near the source of bamboo raw materials.

NER can leverage its geographic and cultural proximity with neighboring countries, especially Bangladesh, which is now the largest source of medical tourists to India, to build up its medical services and medical tourism industry. Guwahati, where medical services are better developed than in any other NER city and private sector participation is significant and growing, is best placed to develop into a medical tourism cluster in the region; other NER cities, like Agartala, can participate in the industry by plugging into the Guwahati cluster.

In the medical tourism industry, the segment catering to long-duration complex services, such as cancer care and neurological treatment, is associated with the high-impact value chain. Such medical services may require frequent hospital stays of short duration spanning several months. Even after the patient returns home, medical care is needed, and, in cases such as cancer and organ transplants, patient monitoring and medical treatment continue throughout the patient's life. The overall size of the margin is typically larger than that in the other strategic segments, due to the longer duration of services. Further, margins are likely to be more equitably shared across the value chain and down the workforce pyramid. Patients spend substantial time outside the destination hospital, which allows other service providers—such as hotels, guest houses, homestays, restaurants, and local transportation providers—to create value by providing services. Given the need for aftercare and patient monitoring for a longer time back at home, hospitals in the source country can also create more value for themselves. The margins are also likely to be better shared down the workforce pyramid, whether in hospitals, hotels, or other service organizations. In hospitals, the coordinated skills of a team of doctors and equipment technicians provide treatment and the requisite clinical experience, while everyone in the workforce, including nurses and ward staff, contribute to creating the desired patient experience by offering compassionate, patient-centered care. In hotels and other service organizations, everyone in the workforce down to the bottom of the pyramid is involved in creating value through the patient experience desired by long-duration patients.

In this industry, women account for a relatively high share of the workforce in hospitals (35–45 percent, on average), hospitality sectors (hotels and restaurants), other service organizations (such as travel agents and airlines), as well as supporting institutions (such as colleges for medical, nursing, and paramedical education). There are several avenues for female entrepreneurship in the medical tourism value chain (for instance, in stand-alone diagnostic centers and pathology labs, nursing homes and clinics, guest houses and homestays, and restaurants), and avenues are also available in the long-duration complex services segment. Long-duration complex services also offer entrepreneurial opportunities for women in convalescent homes for medical tourists and home-care nursing services for local patients and medical tourists who stay in hotels, homestays, or rented accommodations—a cooperative of nurses could, for instance, come together to provide such services.

Bangladesh can play an important role in the development of all the high-impact value chains described in this annex 1A, which will also bring gains to its consumers and firms (box 1.1).

ANNEX 1B: VALUE CHAIN INTERVENTIONS AND FARMER EMPOWERMENT FOR GREATER RETURNS—EXAMPLE FROM A WORLD BANK PROJECT IN HAITI

A transformative initiative that will strengthen the competitiveness of fresh fruit value chains in Haiti is currently under way through a World Bank project (Duch Navarro 2019), with technical input from Wageningen University & Research (WUR).[5] Haitian mangoes fetch about $2 per piece in U.S. supermarkets, of which Haitian farmers receive only $0.02–$0.05; about $0.80 accrues to intermediaries, and the rest is taken up by transportation costs and the profit margins of retailers (WUR 2018). The objective of the initiative is to enable small-scale farmers in some of the poorest parts of Haiti (where the poverty rate exceeds 60 percent) to export high-quality fresh produce, such as mangoes and avocados, to markets in the United States, sell directly without intermediaries, and earn higher returns.

Developing a high-impact fruit value chain, which generates high returns that can also subsequently be more equitably shared with farmers, requires production and delivery of a high-quality, ready-to-eat product,[6] with its freshness intact, to supermarkets in high-value markets comprising discerning customers. The premium on fruit such as avocados in the ready-to-eat refrigerated value chain is almost 40 percent over regular avocados (Fruman and Kim 2015). Attaining such premiums requires a complete restructuring of the existing value chain in Haiti, going all the way back to the agricultural practices employed on farms. For instance, a WUR analysis revealed that if farmers picked mangoes at the optimal time, ensuring that they are mature at harvest but ripen only after they have been transported to the export destination, then many more mangoes would reach the market without having gone bad (WUR 2018). The fruit must be harvested without bruising, which can reduce the value. Less waste along with better premiums fetched by ready-to-eat fruit in efficient markets improves farmer incomes. Experts from WUR have drawn up detailed standard operating procedures for farmers and service providers to follow during cultivation and harvest and thereafter, to ensure that the harvested fruit is consistently of high quality and its quality is preserved all the way from farm to market.

One of the key requirements of this high-impact value chain is an end-to-end cold chain that keeps the fruit in a temperature- and humidity-controlled environment, starting immediately after harvest, until it reaches the consumer. The avocados are put into a cold chamber within three hours of being picked, kept at 4 degrees Celsius until they reach the destination unripened, ripened in a ripening chamber at the destination, and then delivered to local supermarkets (Fruman and Kim 2015). The cold chain preserves freshness and minimizes waste of the product through spoilage while being transported to distant markets of quality-conscious customers. But Haiti currently does not have cold logistics for fresh produce. The World Bank project has been preparing the terrain to attract private sector investors to provide the common services—such as quality control, cold chain logistics, and packing—that are needed for local producers to access more profitable markets. The project also reduces the investment risk to fourth-party logistics service providers,[7] by providing a guarantee of payment as long as service has been provided and products are exported successfully. In this private sector solution, the challenge of aggregation and collection is addressed by the private sector logistics service provider, which is contracted to collect the fruit from the orchard and transport it to the United States, carrying out all the necessary steps for quality control and traceability using blockchain.

The most significant step in empowering farmers under this initiative is the introduction of blockchain for end-to-end traceability and payments. Application of blockchain technology in agriculture has the potential to create transparency, reduce operational costs, and improve food safety, while also improving inclusiveness. Blockchain tracking and payment technology is disrupting the balance of bargaining power between farmers, aggregators, and consumers. The farmers can track the fruit on its journey from farm to market and maintain ownership of their product, without intermediaries, until final sale in the destination market. Farmers are paid directly through smart contracts using phone-based payment systems. In this system, "any intermediaries not adding value disappear unless they provide a much-needed service at a reasonable cost."[8] Although farmers bear the entrepreneurial risk, they also reap greater rewards, as margins that were earlier appropriated by intermediaries and local exporters revert back to the farmers.[9] Tracking technology allows environmentally conscious and socially responsible consumers, who are able and willing to pay more for high-quality products that meet their criteria, to select their purchases while being assured of safety and freshness. Fresh produce is tagged from farm to table, by affixing a quick response (QR) code on boxes of fruit immediately after harvest, which enables shipments to be tracked all the way to the consumer. The QR code, on being scanned, provides access to information about the specific grower and the harvesting location, the temperature at which it is transported from farm to market, as well as the costs and margins at each step in the value chain from the moment the fruit is picked from the tree until the moment it is paid for by the buyer.[10] The real-time data on the whole value chain made available by the blockchain will make the market more transparent and efficient.

In May 2018, a pilot exercise was conducted by the government of Haiti, with support from the World Bank and technical input from WUR. The exercise sent sample shipments to the United States, Canada, and the Netherlands, with data registered in a mock-up distributed ledger. The pilot yielded encouraging results.[11] First, spoilage rates declined dramatically, from up to 60 percent previously, while the quality of the produce and shelf life improved due to better post-harvest handling and temperature-controlled transportation. Second, farmers' revenue increased eightfold with the elimination of intermediate resellers and reductions in markups. Third, real-time data that tracked shipments through their journey from farm to market were available to all parties, including the government. Further, consumers could obtain information about the product by scanning a QR code. The government of Haiti is developing the pilot scaled-up solution.

NOTES

1. NER comprises all states of India to the north and east of the Indian state of West Bengal.
2. Every sector comprises several strategic segments; a strategic segment consists of a particular product variation targeting a specific user or consumer type. Each strategic segment has a unique value chain. Hence, every sector has as many value chains as strategic segments—businesses require different capabilities to compete successfully in the different value chains.
3. "Orders and Guidelines on Imports of Food Articles," Food Safety and Standards Authority of India, New Delhi, http://fssai.gov.in/home/imports/order-guidelines.html (accessed May 30, 2019).
4. A pallet is a unit loading device consisting of a portable, horizontal, rigid platform used as a base for operations in logistics. In other regions, pallets are widely used to conveniently facilitate the storage, stacking, handling, and transportation of goods.
5. WUR is well known for its application-oriented and field-based research on sustainable innovations in fresh food value chains and logistics solutions.
6. Ready-to-eat fruit refers to fruit that is neither underripe nor overripe when it reaches the consumer; it is ready for consumption right away.
7. A fourth-party logistics service provider is a "supply chain integrator that assembles and manages the resources, capabilities, and technology of its own organization with those of complementary service providers to deliver a comprehensive supply chain solution" (Vitasek 2013, 86).
8. Open Access Government (2019).
9. See the video on the World Bank initiative in Haiti, YouTube (accessed April 5, 2019), https://m.youtube.com/watch?feature=youtu.be&v=xpKe8J2i0Wo.
10. Open Access Government (2019); video on the World Bank initiative in Haiti, YouTube (accessed April 5, 2019), https://m.youtube.com/watch?feature=youtu.be&v=xpKe8J2i0Wo.
11. World Bank (2019); YouTube video on the World Bank initiative in Haiti (accessed April 5, 2019), https://m.youtube.com/watch?feature=youtu.be&v=xpKe8J2i0Wo.

REFERENCES

Duch Navarro, Emiliano. 2019. "Haiti Business Development and Investment Project." Disclosable Restructuring Paper P123974, World Bank, Washington, DC, http://documents.worldbank.org/curated/en/338511550943869352/Disclosable-Restructuring-Paper-Haiti-Business-Development-and-Investment-Project-P123974.

Fruman, C., and M. Kim. 2015. "If I Knew Avocados Had More Value I Would Plant More of Them." December 17. http://blogs.worldbank.org/psd/if-i-knew-avocados-had-value-i-would-plant-more-them.

Gitau, C. 2019. "Developing Inclusive Cross-Border Value Chains in North East India: Spices." In *Strengthening Cross-Border Value Chains: Opportunities for India and Bangladesh*, ed. Sanjay Kathuria and Priya Mathur, chapter 1. World Bank, Washington, DC.

Government of India. 2008. *North Eastern Region Vision 2020*. New Delhi: Ministry of Development of North Eastern Region and North Eastern Council, Government of India. http://www.mdoner.gov.in/sites/default/files/silo2_content/ner_vision/Vision_2020.pdf.

———. 2017. *Export of Health Services: A Primary Survey*. New Delhi: Directorate General of Commercial Intelligence and Statistics, Ministry of Commerce and Industry, Government of India. http://www.dgciskol.nic.in/pdfs/Export_of_Health_Services_Final_Book_Report.pdf.

Kathuria, S., ed. 2018. *A Glass Half Full: The Promise of Regional Trade in South Asia*. Washington, DC: World Bank.

Khanna, A. 2019. "Developing Inclusive Cross-Border Value Chains in North East India: Fruits and Vegetables." In *Strengthening Cross-Border Value Chains: Opportunities for India and Bangladesh*, ed. by Sanjay Kathuria and Priya Mathur, chapter 2. World Bank, Washington, DC.

Manghnani, R. 2019. "Developing Inclusive Cross-Border Value Chains in North East India: Bamboo and Bamboo Products." In *Strengthening Cross-Border Value Chains: Opportunities for India and Bangladesh*, ed. Sanjay Kathuria and Priya Mathur, chapter 3. World Bank, Washington, DC.

Mathur, P. 2019. "Developing Inclusive Cross-Border Value Chains in North East India: Medical Tourism." In *Strengthening Cross-Border Value Chains: Opportunities for India and Bangladesh*, ed. Sanjay Kathuria and Priya Mathur, chapter 4. World Bank, Washington, DC.

Nath, A. 2012. "The Role of Trade and Investment in Improving the Growth Prospects of Tripura: With Reference to Bangladesh." Presentation at Stakeholders Conference: MacArthur's Strategic and Economic Capacity Building Program by the Indian Council for Research on International Economic Relations, July 30. http://icrier.org/pdf/ashish_nath_trade_investment.pdf.

Open Access Government. 2019. "World Bank Blockchain Pilot Sows Fresh Narrative for Haiti's Farmers." World Bank, Washington, DC. https://www.openaccessgovernment.org/world-bank-blockchain-haitis-farmers/61205/.

Vitasek, Kate. 2013. *Supply Chain Management Terms and Glossary* (accessed April 6, 2019), http://cscmp.org/imis0/CSCMP/Educate/SCM_Definitions_and_Glossary_of_Terms/CSCMP/Educate/SCM_Definitions_and_Glossary_of_Terms.aspx?hkey=60879588-f65f-4ab5-8c4b-6878815ef921.86.

World Bank. 2009. *Guide for Assessing Investment Needs in Laboratory Capacities for Managing Food Safety, Plant Health, and Animal Health*. Washington, DC: World Bank.

———. 2019. "Pilot of Distributed Ledger Technology for Traceability and Payment in Haiti's Fresh Fruits Value Chains." World Bank, Washington, DC.

WUR (Wageningen University & Research). 2018. "Improved Mango and Avocado Chain Helps Small Scale Farmers in Haiti." Wageningen, Netherlands. https://www.freshplaza.com/article/2198929/improved-mango-and-avocado-chains-helps-small-scale-farmers-in-haiti/.

2 The Promise of Northeast India

THIRUMALAI G. SRINIVASAN

INTRODUCTION

This chapter describes the lagging development outcomes of the North Eastern Region (NER) of India in per capita growth, poverty reduction, and overall human development indicators. Selected potential economic causes of the region's weak performance are analyzed, such as its poor connectivity to the rest of India, small market size, low population density, and inadequate urbanization. The chapter then discusses the welfare consequences for firms, farms, and households of the main challenge of the region's relative geographic isolation from the rest of India. The welfare consequences include significant barriers to trade, high prices for the goods that the poor buy, and the exodus of workers seeking jobs outside NER. The final section of the chapter peers into the future, after highlighting the key strengths of NER and the rising opportunities for growth. These strengths include its comparative advantage in horticultural crops; a youthful, highly educated workforce with proficiency in English language skills and high female labor force participation; and strong service sector orientation. The dynamic market for food and beverages in India and abroad, which is being affected by changing consumer preferences toward healthful foods such as fresh fruit; the growing role of services in manufacturing; and India's strategic shift to Act East in deepening trade relations with NER's neighbors, such as Bangladesh and the Association of Southeast Asian Nations (ASEAN), are some of the rising opportunities that will make use of NER's key strengths.

DEVELOPMENT OUTCOMES AND POTENTIAL CAUSES

Outcomes

Divergent levels of per capita income

NER fits into the well-known puzzle of divergence of growth rates among Indian states.[1] Growth in per capita real value added in NER, at 4.2 percent per year over 2000–15, is 1 percentage point below the all-India aggregate. Among NER states, Mizoram has sustained a higher growth rate, on par with the all-India rate. Tripura has had a higher pace of growth than the NER average in recent years, at a robust 7 percent per year, while Assam has lagged, at 3.4 percent growth (figure 2.1). In contrast, the newly created state of Uttarakhand, which had a starting income similar to that of NER, has rapidly grown to a pace that tops 9 percent per year, supported by its proximity to the National Capital Region. The state of Uttarakhand has attracted industry by taking advantage of the fiscal incentives enabled by its special category status.[2]

Opportunities for growth differ across the administrative boundaries of states in NER. As firms and workers move freely across state boundaries, household consumption may diverge less. Between 1993–94 and 2011–12, real per capita consumption in NER grew at 1.3 percent per year, compared with 2.1 percent for all-India, a divergence of 0.8 of a percentage point less than that in per capita gross domestic product (GDP).

If the market value for carbon sequestration of the forest cover (which is not part of traditional national accounts) in NER is added,[3] the income gap closes, but only by 4 percent over baseline levels of real gross value added.

Slower pace of poverty reduction

Poverty is estimated to be higher in NER compared with all-India or comparator mountain states (table 2.1; NER states are shown in table 2A.1 in annex 2A). Consistent with the slower pace of growth in real gross state domestic product (GSDP) per capita, the rate of poverty reduction in NER has been slowing in the recent past—it is a fifth of the rate for all of India or the comparators over 2005–12 (table 2.1). In Assam, poverty increased between 2004–05 and 2009–10 but fell sharply in the following two years. In Mizoram, poverty has been rising, and increasingly so, with the share of income of the bottom three quintiles falling

FIGURE 2.1

Per capita real gross value added, 2000–15

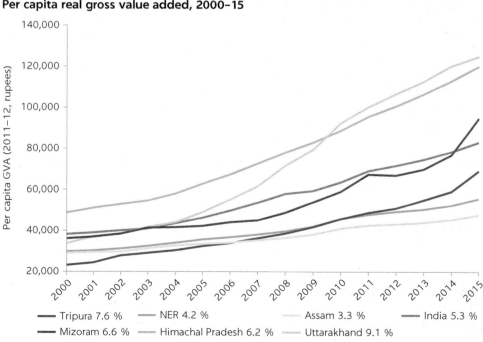

Source: Chain-linked series of different base years available from Ministry of Statistics and Programme Implementation Database, Government of India, New Delh, http://mospi.nic.in/data.
Note: GVA = gross value added.

TABLE 2.1 **Percentage of poor, using Tendulkar poverty lines**
Percent

STATE	1993–94	2004–05	2009–10	2011–12	REDUCTION PER YEAR, 1994–2012	REDUCTION PER YEAR, 2005–12
Assam	52.2	34.4	37.9	32.5	−1.1	−0.2
Mizoram	13.3	15.3	21.1	22.0	0.5	0.8
Tripura	33.1	40.6	17.4	14.9	−1.0	−3.2
NER	**48.8**	**32.2**	**33.6**	**29.0**	**−1.1**	**−0.4**
Memorandum items						
All-India	45.5	37.2	29.8	22.0	−1.3	−1.9
Himachal Pradesh	34.8	22.9	9.5	8.0	−1.5	−1.9
Uttarakhand	—	32.7	18.0	11.4	—	−2.7

Sources: World Bank computations for 1993–94 and 2012; estimates from Government of India (2014) for 2004–05 and 2009–10.
Note: NER = North Eastern Region of India; — = not available.

TABLE 2.2 **Human Development Index Rank**

STATE	1993	1999–2000	2004–05	2009–10	2011–12
Assam	21	25	22	22	26
Mizoram	3	4	8	10	13
Tripura	14	15	17	12	14
NER (range)	**3–22**	**4–25**	**8–22**	**10–23**	**13–27**
Memorandum items					
Himachal Pradesh	7	5	4	3	3
Uttarakhand	—	22	20	14	11

Source: Mukherjee, Chakraborty, and Sikdar 2014.
Note: The ranks are among a consistent set of 28 states over the whole period. — = not available.

over time. The growth in GSDP reported for Mizoram does not appear to be benefiting the poor. Tripura is an exception to the trend for the region; it has reduced poverty at a pace faster than that of the comparators.

Slide in Human Development Index Rank
Use of a broader measure of welfare, as indicated by the Human Development Index—a composite of per capita consumption, educational attainment up to Class XI, and health (mortality) outcomes—also indicates a slide in ranks over the long term (table 2.2 and, for all states, table 2A.2 in annex 2A). Mizoram has conceded its early lead of rank 3 and Assam has fallen to rank 26 of a possible 28. Tripura has maintained its near-median rank of 14. The other mountain states, Himachal Pradesh and Uttarakhand, unlike NER, have been rising in rank, in part helped by booming state economies.

Potential economic causes of weak outcomes

Poor connectivity
The transport connectivity of NER states to the rest of India and Bangladesh was disrupted by the 1947 partition. NER's land connection to the rest of India shrank to a thin, 17-mile-wide corridor at the narrowest point, and the newly

demarcated international border with Bangladesh began to restrict the flow of goods and people. In contrast, along India's borders with Nepal and Bhutan, there is freer movement of people (neither visit visas nor work permits are required). This disruption piled further connectivity handicaps on most NER states, which already had a geographic challenge of mountainous terrain, with the share of hill districts ranging from 50 to 100 percent except in Assam. The *thick* or *hard* international borders are the unique history of NER, unlike other landlocked states in India. Over 40 percent of the total perimeters of NER state boundaries and nearly 90 percent of NER's international borders are hard borders (table 2.3). Moving people and goods across hard borders can take days, not hours. In contrast, the landlocked mountain states of Himachal Pradesh and Uttarakhand do not have human-made hard borders along their perimeter. These burdens weigh heavily on NER growth and poverty, offsetting the gains in the human capital achievements of its people and the richness of its natural resources.

Concerted efforts to bridge the transport infrastructure gap in NER have gained significant momentum in recent years. Investments have been made to expand and improve the road and railway networks, activate waterways, and operationalize more airports. The focus has been on improving connectivity within NER, between NER and the rest of India, and between NER and neighboring countries (see chapter 3 for details).

Connectivity outcomes within NER states improved significantly during 2000 to 2015. In every state in NER, the median time to reach the nearest city, computed using geographic information system (GIS) data, was cut from more than three hours in 2000 to an hour by 2015. The reduction should be taken as indicative rather than precise because the definition of city had changed.[4] This reduction is sharper than the reduction for all-India, in which median travel time fell from 2 to 1.5 hours (figure 2.2). For Assam and Tripura, the time to reach the

TABLE 2.3 **Burden of hard borders for NER states**

Percent

STATE	HARD BORDERS' SHARE OF THE PERIMETER	HARD BORDERS' SHARE OF INTERNATIONAL BORDERS
Assam	8.4	49.6
Manipur	42.9	100.0
Meghalaya	37.7	100.0
Mizoram	76.7	100.0
Nagaland	20.1	100.0
Sikkim	48.2	62.9
Tripura	91.6	100.0
NER	**40.5**	**88.7**
Himachal Pradesh	21.4	100.0
Uttarakhand	19.4	46.8

Sources: Data for NER states are from Ministry of Development of NER, http://mdoner.gov.in; data for others are from QuickGS.com, http://www.quickgs.com/indian-state-with-maximum-international -borders/.
Note: Borders facing Nepal and Bhutan are classified as soft and the rest as hard, corresponding to the ease of access for people and goods in crossing the international borders.

FIGURE 2.2
Median travel time to the nearest city

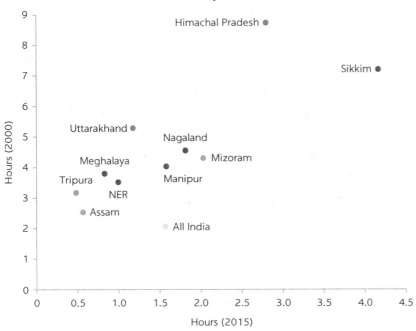

Source: Weiss et al. 2018.
Note: Based on Global Access to Cities GIS data. The time is measured for the least-cost path taken to reach the nearest city from every place in the state (250 square meter tiles) by road, rail, or water.

nearest city was cut to 30 minutes. However, Mizoram residents travel two hours to reach the nearest city. The outlier is Sikkim. Using this definition, a comparable mountainous state, Himachal Pradesh, has worse internal connectivity than most NER states.

The connectivity of NER states to the nearest Indian seaport is comparable to other mountain states in India. The time it takes people in NER states to reach the nearest Indian port is comparable to that in the other landlocked mountain states, Himachal Pradesh and Uttarakhand (figure 2.3). Residents of Assam can reach the Port of Kolkata more quickly than residents of Himachal Pradesh and Uttarakhand can reach Kandla, their nearest port.

NER states are at a major disadvantage in reaching the market of the National Capital Region or other growth hubs compared with other mountain states. It takes at least 25 hours for people in the NER states to reach Delhi, compared with about five hours for people in Uttarakhand and Himachal Pradesh, according to Google Maps. More sophisticated measures of connectivity (such as betweenness and eigenvalue), which measure whether NER nodal cities lie on busy corridors or connect with other well-connected nodes, are likely to show an even more adverse picture of connectivity for NER.[5]

Market size

NER states together are home to about 45 million people, which is comparable in size to Andhra Pradesh (after the Telangana split), with Assam the most populous, at 31 million in 2011. As a region, the size of the market appears to be comparable to other large Indian states. Population growth has been decelerating, as in the rest of India, to 1.6 percent annual growth during the decade ending

FIGURE 2.3

Travel time to the nearest port, 2015

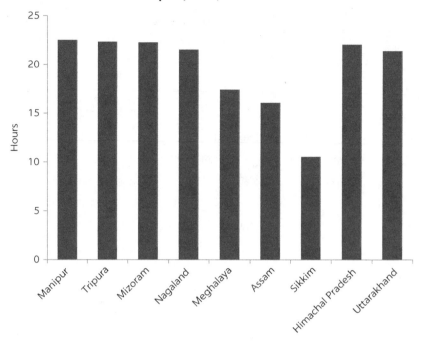

Source: Weiss et al. 2018.
Note: Based on "friction surface" used for building Global Access to Cities GIS data. The time is measured for the least-cost path taken to reach the nearest city from every place in the state (250 square meter tiles) by road, rail, or water.

in 2011. Although India is projected to reach the replacement level of fertility rate of 2.1 in 2020, most NER states are in a slower transition to that goal. However, net out-migration of the working-age population could reduce population growth, a likely issue for smaller states like Nagaland and Sikkim.

Population density

It is difficult to reap the benefits of agglomeration if the population remains scattered over a large area. A crude measure of agglomeration is population density, but merely dividing the population by area (inhabited and uninhabited) gives a misleading picture of population density. Measuring net population density—the population over area settled for human activity (leaving out forests, wasteland, and so forth)—shows that NER states have net densities comparable to, or higher than, Himachal Pradesh and Uttarakhand (figure 2.4). Assam and Tripura have net densities comparable to the average for India, at around 400 persons per square kilometer. Mizoram has a much lower density, at 50 persons per square kilometer. Other NER states—such as Manipur, Meghalaya, and Nagaland—compare well with rapidly growing Himachal Pradesh.

Only parts of Assam, Tripura, and Sikkim are urbanizing rapidly

Urbanization is associated with growth and poverty reduction. The clustering of people and firms in urban areas creates opportunities for specialization, scale,

FIGURE 2.4

Net population density

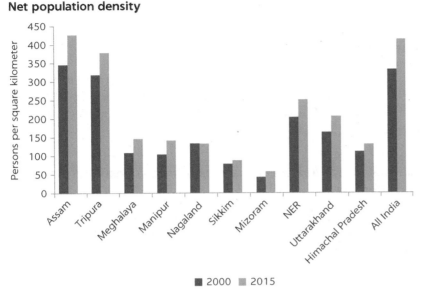

■ 2000 ■ 2015

Source: World Bank computations using Global Human Settlement Database (European Commission), European Union (accessed 2016), https://ghsl.jrc.ec.europa.eu/data.php.

and spillover of knowledge. Rural areas also benefit from the large, dense markets for their products, with an ensuing reduction in poverty. Measuring urbanization, however, has been problematic. The traditional measures based on the census are affected by the reclassification of rural areas to urban.[6] Use of remote-sensing-based agglomeration measures has improved the census-based measurement of urbanization that looked at the population count, density, and share of the nonfarm workforce.

Census measures tend to underestimate the extent of urbanization. Based on the 2011 census, NER is lagging in urbanization: one in five NER residents lived in urban areas compared with one in three for all-India. After a sharp rise in the preceding decade, the share of urban population in NER leveled off during 2001–11. Tripura and Sikkim were the notable exceptions, where the shares increased. Mizoram was the most urbanized, with half the population living in urban areas. However, remote-sensing-based measures tell a more nuanced story.[7] Using the high-density cluster[8] definition of the European Commission Science Hub, NER's average urbanization difference with all-India is much narrower: 58 percent (NER) versus 63 percent (all-India) in 2015. Assam improves its rank by 22 places compared with the census-based measure, while Mizoram drops by an equal number of places. Alternatively, using nighttime lights remotely sensed from satellites, the intensity of light is seen to be increasing and spreading wider. Between 2000 and 2013, the twin cities of Tinsukia and Dibrugarh, the Guwahati metropolitan area, the neighborhood of Agartala in Tripura, and Gangtok in Sikkim outpaced the rest of NER in luminosity and its spread.

WELFARE CONSEQUENCES OF GEOGRAPHIC ISOLATION

All the NER states are landlocked, have a predominantly mountainous terrain, and hug a hard international border. These geographic features restrict access to the large domestic market in India, adjacent countries, and the wider world. The high transport costs of reaching NER areas worsen the terms of trade of the local economies: imported products cost more, and locally produced goods lose competitiveness as they are transported over long distances. Households pay higher prices for consumption goods, and firms pay an implicit transport tax on inputs imported into the region and goods exported out of the region. Higher input costs reduce value addition, diminishing productivity and real wages. This section quantifies the effects of geographic isolation on NER economies from barriers to trade and higher consumer prices for the poor.

NER states face formidable barriers to trade, mostly across state borders

Infrastructure barriers to international trade can be costlier for states that are further from seaports—the predominant way goods are traded internationally. The value of NER states' exports was only about $500 million, or 0.2 percent of all Indian exports, in 2015–16 and 2016–17.[9]

A recent study estimates NER states' trade barriers to be very high, exceeded only by those of the mountain states of Himachal Pradesh and Uttarakhand (Van Leemput 2016). The study computes trade barriers separately for exports and imports for agriculture and manufacturing. The total barrier (domestic and international) is the relative price of local to international prices, with the wedge implicitly covering transport, logistics, tariffs and paratariffs, and other costs of weak governance. Since NER states are predominantly agricultural, it is instructive to compare Indian states by barriers to agricultural exports. The estimated total barrier for agricultural exports varies from 2.1 in Delhi to 13.4 in Himachal Pradesh. NER states average 9.5, with Meghalaya leading at 12.5. The total barriers to exports consist of a common external barrier for all states at 2.1 and state-specific internal barriers. On average, landlocked states face internal barriers that are five times higher than those of states with a port. For NER states, on average, internal barriers account for three-quarters of the total barriers to agricultural exports, varying between 69 and 81 percent, reducing their competitiveness in exporting agricultural goods (figure 2.5). The study breaks down internal

FIGURE 2.5

Share of internal barriers to agricultural exports by state, 2011–12

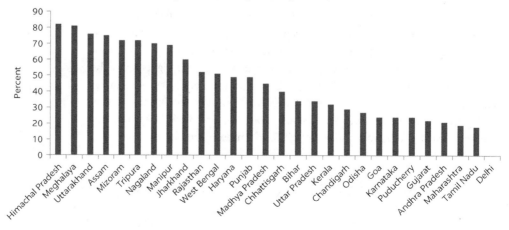

Source: Based on data from Van Leemput 2016.

barriers as the sum of barriers from rural to urban areas within a state plus inter-state barriers cumulated over every state that goods must cross to reach the near-est seaport. The interstate barriers include shipping costs, central sales taxes, and octrois (entry taxes).[10]

The internal barriers to exports in Assam, Tripura, and Mizoram, the focus states of this report, are higher than those of the nearest state with a seaport, West Bengal, by several orders of magnitude, and more so in agriculture than manufacturing (figure 2.6). Assam has the highest barriers among the three states, apparently because it has a higher rural-urban barrier than the other two. Manufacturing barriers are lower than those in agriculture, because by assump-tion all manufacturing is concentrated in urban areas, which avoids the need for transport costs from rural regions.

Bringing down interstate barriers will have high payoffs for NER states. The median cross-state barrier in India is five times bigger than that in the United States, a country that is three times as large. In India, the median cross-state price differential for goods is 150 percent, compared with 30 percent in the United States.[11] If cross-state barriers in India were to come down to the levels of those in the United States, landlocked north and northeast states in India would have the most to gain in welfare. Assam would gain moderately (1–5 percent), and Mizoram would gain the most (35–50 percent). Tripura's gains would be at an intermediate level, in the range of 15–25 percent.[12]

A big step was taken on July 1, 2017, to lower the cross-state barriers by the implementation of the goods and services tax (GST), which has replaced a cas-cading tier of many individual state and central taxes. Any erosion of prevailing tax incentives for firms *already located* in NER states because of the tax regime change has been restored to the incentive levels that prevailed before the intro-duction of the GST.[13] The incentives expire 10 years after the commencement of commercial production for eligible units that commenced operations before the introduction of the GST. The GST lowers cross-state barriers in three clear ways: a lower average tax rate at destination states; fewer compliance costs; and fewer

FIGURE 2.6

Differences in trade barriers between Assam, Tripura, Mizoram, and West Bengal

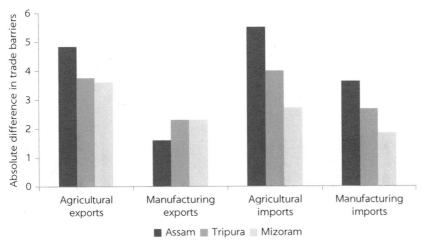

Source: Based on data from Van Leemput 2016.
Note: The bars in this figure represent absolute difference compared to barriers faced by West Bengal.

holdups in clearing while goods cross state borders. Most respondents to a 2018 Federation of Indian Chambers of Commerce and Industry survey of GST implementation confirmed the ease of transporting goods across state borders and the savings in trucking time (FICCI 2018). Most savings in time and cost come from long-haul routes. The typical truck carrying goods from Assam to Delhi, for example, would now save five hours of waiting at checkpoints (MORTH 2017). The estimated welfare effects suggest that the gain in welfare for landlocked states is 2–3 percent (Van Leemput and Wiencek 2017). Mizoram would gain 7–12 percent, and Assam and Tripura would gain a more moderate 2–4 percent (Van Leemput and Wiencek 2017).

Poor people in NER face higher prices

State-specific poverty lines estimated by the Expert Groups on poverty can be used to measure the price divergence across states for households. The underlying prices for the products that go into the basic-needs basket are derived from "unit values" observed at the local level during the consumer expenditure surveys that collect the values and quantities of goods purchased by households. In 2012 and 2014, respectively, the Tendulkar and Rangarajan committee Expert Groups followed the same method to derive state-specific poverty lines.

Using West Bengal, the nearest Indian state with access to a seaport, unlike landlocked NER, as the comparator, the rural poor all over NER face higher poverty lines. The rural poor in Nagaland fare the worst, facing a poverty line 60 percent higher than that in West Bengal (figure 2.7). The rural poor in Mizoram face the highest poverty line among Assam, Mizoram, and Tripura. Tripura shows the least markup over West Bengal. Other mountain states in the North—Himachal Pradesh and Uttarakhand—have poverty lines only slightly higher than that in Assam.

Higher poverty line divergences for rural than urban areas compared with West Bengal echo the earlier discussion on trade barriers—the greater the

FIGURE 2.7

It is costlier to be poor in NER states, especially in rural areas

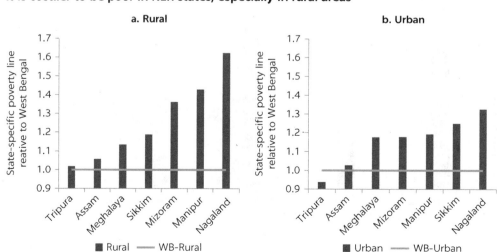

Source: State-specific poverty lines based on data from Government of India 2014.
Note: WB = West Bengal.

distance that goods need to move in the interior, the higher the costs. If Mizoram had poverty lines equal to the average of Assam and Tripura, a reduction of 20 percent, poverty in Mizoram would drop from 22 to 8 percent.

NER workers are migrating to nearby states and fast-growing, far-flung states

Seeking jobs and better pay, workers are increasingly on the move.[14] Eventually, their spouses and children follow. This section focuses on out-of-state NER migration; *intrastate* migration is subsumed under urbanization, which is discussed elsewhere in this section. Over 2001–11, net interstate migration was positive (more people moving in than leaving) in Meghalaya, Sikkim, and Tripura; it was negative in Assam, Mizoram, Manipur, and Nagaland (table 2.4). For NER as a region, there was a net outflow of about 100,000 persons every decade, only about 0.3 percent of the population at the beginning of the decade. Outward-bound migrants from NER gravitate to the nearby states of West Bengal and Bihar. The next favorite destinations are the farther-away but faster-growing states around Delhi, Maharashtra, Karnataka, and Andhra Pradesh.

NER female out-migration differs from that of the rest of India

Migration analysis in India shows that, for internal migration, most migrants are female (70 percent), and 91 percent of rural women and 61 percent of urban women migrate for marriage (UNICEF 2012). NER states, except Assam, provide a stark contrast to the rest of India. The economic motives of employment and studies play a significant role in female migrants out of NER. Meghalaya is at the top of all states and national territories in India. Nearly half or more of the women migrants from Meghalaya, Manipur, and Mizoram leave to work or study (figure 2.8). Residents of the other mountain states, Himachal Pradesh and Uttarakhand, do not migrate as often.

TABLE 2.4 **NER's net interstate migration**

STATE	2001		2011	
	NUMBER	RATE (%)	NUMBER	RATE (%)
Sikkim	16,281	2.9	15,853	4.0
Meghalaya	13,276	0.5	12,598	0.7
Tripura	16,724	0.5	16,871	0.6
Assam	−159,707	−0.6	−154,118	−0.7
Mizoram	−9,140	−1.1	−9,463	−1.3
Manipur	−26,338	−1.2	−25,477	−1.4
Nagaland	−18,263	−0.9	−17,647	−1.5
NER	**−107,885**	**−0.3**	**−104,376**	**−0.3**

Sources: Census of India 2011, table D12; Census of India 2001, Data Highlights; calculations based on place of residence over the previous 0–9 years.
Note: Interstate migration includes migration to other NER states. For example, Assam lost 154,118 persons, of whom 58,918 left for destinations within NER. NER as a region, reported in the last row, is the sum of the eight states. "Rate" refers to migration as a percentage of the population at the start of the decade. NER = North Eastern Region.

FIGURE 2.8
Reasons for out-migration of females, 2007–08

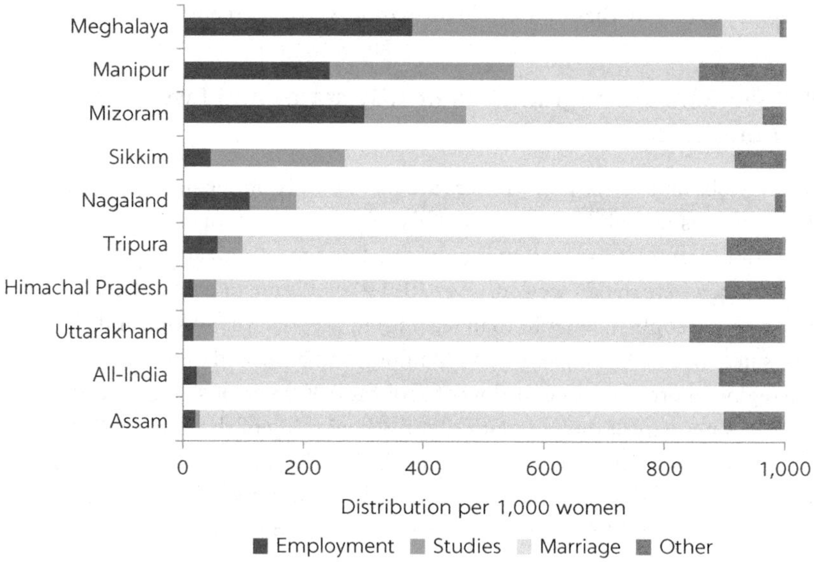

Distribution per 1,000 women

■ Employment ■ Studies ▨ Marriage ■ Other

Source: NSS 2008, table 6.3.1.

LEVERAGING NER'S STRENGTHS FOR HIGHER GROWTH AND MORE INCLUSION

NER states should play to their many strengths to overcome the hurdle of geographic isolation

The key advantages of the NER states are their agroclimatic endowments and the service orientation of the economy. The latter is reflected in their youthful and literate population, high female labor force participation rates, and proficiency in English. These strengths can be leveraged to open new avenues for high-value growth. NER can use its strengths to participate in the dynamic market for the food and beverages segment of the fast-moving consumer goods market in India and abroad, which is being affected by changing consumer preferences toward healthful foods and the "servicification" and "servitization" (as defined in the last section of this chapter) of manufacturing and skill-intensive service sectors such as medical tourism.

NER states have varying degrees of comparative advantage in horticultural crops

The agroclimatic zones in NER vary from tropical in the plains of the Brahmaputra Valley to alpine hills. Hills dominate the region outside the Brahmaputra Valley, with lush green forests and copious rain. As a result of the hilly terrian, NER is not self-sufficient in producing rice—the staple food grain of the inhabitants—or legumes, but the region has 53 percent marketable surplus in fruit production (Roy et al. 2016).

Table 2.5 shows the pattern of the revealed comparative advantage (RCA) of NER states in 2013–14 in growing six horticultural subgroup crops: fruits, spices,

TABLE 2.5 **Revealed comparative advantage in horticultural crops, 2013–14**

STATE	HORTICULTURE	FRUITS	SPICES	VEGETABLES	PLANTATION CROPS	MEDICINAL PLANTS	FLOWERS
Assam	0.8	0.8	1.1	1.2	1.0	0.3	0.5
Manipur	2.6	2.0	0.9	0.7	0.1	—	0.8
Meghalaya	0.2	1.0	1.1	0.9	1.4	—	0.0
Mizoram	2.9	1.5	1.3	0.8	0.4	0.4	0.1
Nagaland	2.2	1.5	0.8	1.1	0.1	—	0.0
Sikkim	5.4	0.7	3.3	0.9	0.0	—	0.3
Tripura	2.3	1.7	0.3	0.9	0.8	—	0.0
NER	**0.6**	**1.2**	**1.1**	**0.9**	**0.7**	**0.4**	**0.3**
Himachal Pradesh	2.8	2.3	0.2	0.7	0.0	0.2	0.2
Uttarakhand	2.0	2.1	0.2	0.8	0.0	—	0.5

Sources: State crop areas are derived from Open Government Data Platform India (All India and State Wise Area and Production of Various Horticulture Crops), Ministry of Electronics and Information Technology, Government of India, https://data.gov.in/catalog/all-india-and-state-wise-area-and-production -various-horticulture-crops; land utilization data are derived from Government of India 2017a.
Note: For horticultural products as a group—which includes fruits and vegetables, spices, flowers, plantation crops, and medicinal plants—revealed comparative advantage (RCA) is shown with respect to the gross cropped area of the state as a proxy for potential production. For each horticultural crop subgroup (fruits, spices, vegetables, plantation crops, medicinal and aromatic plants, and flowers), the RCA is shown with respect to all areas under horticulture as a group. RCA is the ratio of percentage of gross cropped area (GCA) under the crop in a state to the percentage of GCA under the crop for all-India. — = not available.

vegetables, plantation crops, medicinal and aromatic plants, and flowers. The general pattern emerges that NER states have strengths in growing fruits and spices. Further, given the low penetration of chemical fertilizers and pesticides in NER, the horticultural produce from the region is typically organic or near-organic. Fruits and spices are high-value crops, and organic produce is even more so; their demand tends to rise with the growth in incomes of consumers.

NER states have a strong service sector orientation

The share of the service (or tertiary) sector in GDP in most NER states has been at or above the median for all states in India (48.6 percent), ranging from 51 percent in Tripura to 63 percent in Manipur; Sikkim is an exception. NER states stand out compared with the 35 percent share of services in other mountain states. The tertiary sector contributes roughly half the GSDP and is the dominant sector in the three focus states in NER; the share of the primary sector is second, at 30 percent; and the secondary sector constitutes the remaining 20 percent. Although superficially the three focus states appear to have similar shares (figure 2.9; and, in annex 2A, table 2A.3 for GSDP and table 2A.4 for employment), the underlying subsectors differ in their importance. Assam has a larger mining (petroleum) subsector in the primary sector and larger manufacturing and trade sectors. Mizoram has negligible manufacturing but more electricity generation and a large public administration service sector. Tripura has more diversified sources of growth in nonagriculture sectors. With respect to employment, half the share is in the primary sector, except in Tripura. The high share of the secondary sector in Tripura results from labor-intensive construction activities. The service sector appears to have higher value added per person. Annex 2B provides a more detailed analysis of the structure of GSDP for all the NER states.

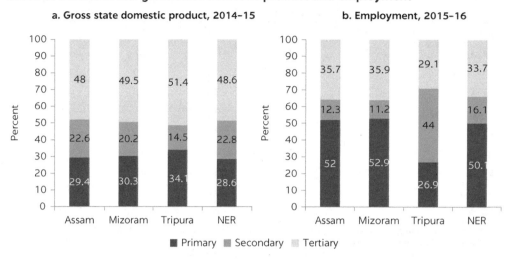

Sources: Gross State Domestic Product of NE States (database), North Eastern Development Finance Corporation Ltd., https://databank.nedfi.com/content/gross-state-domestic-product-ne-states; National Sample Survey Fifth Employment-Unemployment Survey, Labor Bureau, Government of India.
Note: NER = North Eastern Region.

NER states have a large, youthful, and highly literate workforce with relatively high female labor force participation

The working-age population (ages 15 and older) constitutes two-thirds of the total. Youth (ages 15–24) form a fifth of the population, numbering about six million in 2011. Adult literacy for the male workers in Tripura and Mizoram is in the top quartile among all states in India; for females, adult literacy in most NER states is in the top two quartiles (table 2A.5 in annex 2A). NER's labor force participation rate is higher than the all-India average for males and strikingly more so for females. The labor force participation rate for the population ages 15 years and older is over 80 percent for males and 50 percent for females (figure 2.10). Female labor force participation tends to be higher in Mizoram and Tripura. Male youth have higher labor force participation rates, at nearly 70 percent, but only half the young women work or seek work, in part because they seek higher education, as in Mizoram. Young women's labor force participation is higher in Tripura. Five percent of the working-age population in Tripura has completed secondary school, and the rate is higher still in Mizoram, at 7 percent. The labor force participation rates for the NER states are provided in table 2A.6 in annex 2A.

English proficiency is high, especially in the hill states of NER

An important asset for youth who seek to be employed in professional services is English language proficiency. In NER states, particularly the four hill states, English has been a medium of instruction in primary schools for many years. Historically, Roman script has been used to transcribe various vernacular spoken languages, giving the literate a head start in reading English. Because of the supportive environment for English, NER states (other than Assam and Tripura) have maintained high ranks in English test achievement in Class X examinations (table 2.6). The mean absolute scores show very little difference between boys and girls or rural and urban settings.

FIGURE 2.10

Labor force participation rates, 2011

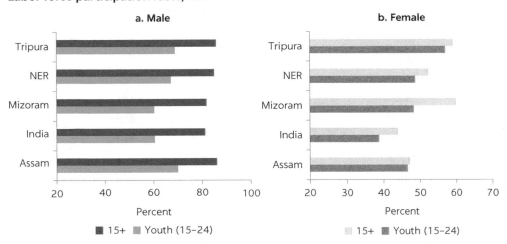

Source: Table Series B-1, Census of India 2011, http://www.censusindia.gov.in/DigitalLibrary/Tables.aspx.
Note: Labor force participation rate is the ratio of the sum of main workers, marginal workers, marginal workers seeking work, and nonworkers seeking work, as a share of the population in the relevant age group.

TABLE 2.6 **Class X examination achievement in English, rank among states and national territories, 2015**

STATE, NATIONAL TERRITORY, OR BOARD	MEAN ACHIEVEMENT	GENDER		AREA	
		BOYS	GIRLS	RURAL	URBAN
Nagaland	1	1	1	1	1
Mizoram	3	3	3	3	5
Sikkim	4	4	4	4	3
Meghalaya	5	5	5	7	4
Assam	17	16	18	16	26
Tripura	21	20	21	20	18
Memorandum items					
Himachal Pradesh	22	22	23	22	19
Uttarakhand	22	23	22	22	21

Source: National Achievement Survey Class X, 2015, National Council of Educational Research and Training, http://www.ncert.nic.in/programmes/NAS/NAS.html.
Note: Thirty-one states and national territories reported achievement levels. Five states—Bihar, Chhattisgarh, Jharkhand, Manipur, and Uttar Pradesh—are not reported.

NER states employ proportionately more women in nonagricultural work

Although the share of women in the primary sector in NER is similar to the all-India and mountain state shares, NER stands out in female labor force participation in the nonprimary sectors (table 2.7). In the secondary sector, a third of the employed are women, and in services almost a quarter are women. In NER in the primary sector, Nagaland and Mizoram have high shares of female employment, at nearly half. In the secondary sector, the share of women is more than half in Tripura, Sikkim, and Manipur. Women's share

TABLE 2.7 **Share of women employed, 2015–16**

Percent

STATE	PRIMARY	SECONDARY	TERTIARY
Assam	30.0	15.4	19.6
Manipur	34.8	68.1	24.7
Meghalaya	38.0	42.0	45.9
Mizoram	48.8	35.5	39.1
Nagaland	52.4	24.5	30.3
Sikkim	42.4	51.3	22.2
Tripura	20.0	51.3	27.4
NER	**33.2**	**34.6**	**23.2**
Memorandum items			
Himachal Pradesh	32.0	11.5	17.2
Uttarakhand	35.2	14.5	13.6
All-India	35.3	20.7	17.6

Source: Based on the Fifth Survey of Employment and Unemployment (2015–16), Labor Bureau, Government of India, http://labourbureaunew.gov.in/UserContent/EUS_5th_1.pdf.
Note: The distribution of employment across sectors relies on the usual principal and subsidiary status approach. The absolute numbers of males and females employed by sector are derived by first using the projected population as of July 2015 on the worker-to-population ratio for the population ages 15 and over, which is available by gender in the distribution tables. All data are from the Fifth Survey. NER = North Eastern Region.

of tertiary sector employment is 40 percent or more in Mizoram and Meghalaya. In the secondary and tertiary sectors, Assam appears to lag the other NER states.

Worldwide, there is a growing segment of discerning consumers

Discerning consumers value quality and are driven by concerns about their health and the environment and various social causes (such as gender discrimination and use of child labor). They are empowered and better informed. In India, too, this segment of consumers is growing with the rapidly expanding middle class,[15] rising incomes, and growing access to the Internet. The expanding middle class will be exposed to global trends in wellness and social responsibility, influencing what types of products they consume. In the food products segment, health-conscious consumers in India and the rest of the world, backed by higher purchasing power, could follow the government's healthy diet guidelines, which prescribe a diet that includes fruits and vegetables. The World Health Organization's (WHO) dietary guidelines, also followed by India, recommend eating at least 400 grams per day, or five portions, of fruits and vegetables.[16] Micha et al. (2015, 5) find that in 2010, among adults across 187 countries, mean global fruit intake was 81.3 grams per day and mean vegetable intake was 208.8 grams per day;[17] for India, the consumption levels were even lower, at 22.7 grams per day for fruits and 160 grams per day for vegetables. Thus, worldwide, there is a large gap between the actual and recommended consumption of fruits and vegetables. Further, discerning consumers are likely to seek high-quality produce, which is fresh, organically or near-organically produced, and meets other criteria that they value, such as respect for the environment and support for the inclusion of women and other underrepresented groups in production.

Health, environment, and social causes

NER can leverage the growing concern for health, the environment, and social causes, and the associated growth in the segment of discerning consumers, for development opportunities. The region can use its horticultural advantages to cater to the growing demand for fresh fruits, vegetables, and spices, especially those that are grown organically or near-organically, with the significant participation of women. If the challenges along the supply chain from farm to table are overcome, the market potential for NER's horticultural produce remains very significant. Bamboo, which matures quickly, is a green building material that can be sustainably harvested. With its vast bamboo resources, NER can benefit from emerging trends and cater to the environmentally conscious consumer.

The service sector is emerging as an important driver of growth

The service sector's direct contribution to GDP growth has been dominant across India. More than two-thirds of the growth in overall GDP came from the service sector between 2012 and 2016. Further, the sector's indirect contribution to GDP, as services input into manufacturing output (servicification),[18] has also been rising over time. The role of the service sector in trade is much larger than what is typically recorded as service trade. For example, in the exporting of manufactured goods from India, the embodied service content in intermediate input use was nearly 50 percent in 2013 (Lanz and Maurer 2015). The share of value added from different stages in the manufacturing value chain from product design, components manufacturing, assembly, marketing, and after-sale services is visually drawn as the "smile curve." The data show that the share of value added contributed by services to the manufacturing value chain is increasing over time (Hallward-Driemier and Nayyar 2018). In addition, increasingly, manufacturing firms are providing services along with their core products, with such services adding value to the goods postproduction (servitization) (Huria et al. forthcoming). For example, Apple provides its consumers an entire range of services (such as apps from the App Store and music from iTunes) with its phones, computers, iPads, and watches (Huria et al. forthcoming).

There are potential opportunities for NER states that have been strong in services but lag in manufacturing

The share of the service sector in NER has been higher than the median for all states and other mountain states in India. But NER lags in manufacturing. In 2014–15, there were only 107 organized manufacturing establishments (per million population to scale for market) in NER states, compared with 184 for all-India.[19] Within NER, Assam and Tripura are relatively denser as locations for organized manufacturing establishments, but even these two states lack "sophistication"[20] in products produced for their income levels. The lagging sophistication is indicative of murky prospects for future growth in manufacturing. But riding the wave of servicification of manufacturing or services alone offers NER a launchpad to faster growth by using its strengths in service orientation and its literate, youthful, English-speaking workforce. The region can participate in service sectors such as tourism, including medical tourism, education, and information technology and information technology–enabled services. It can also participate in services that serve as inputs into the fast-moving consumer goods and other manufacturing sectors, especially those that can be provided remotely—for example, back-office operations, market research, and call centers for after-sale services.

ANNEX 2A: TABLES

TABLE 2A.1 **Percentage of the poor: Tendulkar poverty lines**

Percent

STATE	1993–94	2004–05	2009–10	2011–12	REDUCTION PER YEAR, 1994–2012	REDUCTION PER YEAR, 2005–12
Assam	52.2	34.4	37.9	32.5	−1.1	−0.2
Manipur	65.2	38.0	47.1	37.1	−1.6	−0.1
Meghalaya	35.9	16.1	17.1	11.8	−1.3	−0.5
Mizoram	13.3	15.3	21.1	22.0	0.5	0.8
Nagaland	20.6	9.0	20.9	18.7	−0.1	1.2
Sikkim	32.0	31.1	13.1	8.8	−1.3	−2.8
Tripura	33.1	40.6	17.4	14.9	−1.0	−3.2
NER	**48.8**	**32.2**	**33.6**	**29.0**	**−1.1**	**−0.4**
Memorandum items						
All-India	45.5	37.2	29.8	22.0	−1.3	−1.9
Himachal Pradesh	34.8	22.9	9.5	8.0	−1.5	−1.9
Uttarakhand	—	32.7	18.0	11.4	—	−2.7

Sources: World Bank computations, 1993–94 and 2012; estimates from "The Expert Group Report to Review the Methodology for the Measurement of Poverty," Planning Commission, Government of India, 2014, 2004–05, and 2009–10.
Note: — = not available.

TABLE 2A.2 **Human Development Index Rank**

STATE	1993	1999–2000	2004–05	2009–10	2011–12
Assam	21	25	22	22	26
Manipur	15	16	19	21	22
Meghalaya	16	18	14	18	20
Mizoram	3	4	8	10	13
Nagaland	6	8	13	17	19
Sikkim	17	19	15	15	15
Tripura	14	15	17	12	14
NER, range	**3–22**	**4–25**	**8–22**	**10–23**	**13–27**
Memorandum items					
Himachal Pradesh	7	5	4	3	3
Uttarakhand	—	22	20	14	11

Source: Mukherjee, Chakraborty, and Sikdar 2014.
Note: The ranks are among a consistent set of 28 states over the whole period. — = not available.

TABLE 2A.3 **Share of gross state domestic product, 2014–15**
Percent

STATE	PRIMARY	SECONDARY	TERTIARY
Assam	29.4	22.6	48.0
Manipur	19.8	17.2	62.9
Meghalaya	23.2	24.7	52.1
Mizoram	30.3	20.2	49.5
Nagaland	32.2	9.6	58.2
Sikkim	8.0	61.2	30.8
Tripura	34.1	14.5	51.4
NER	**28.6**	**22.8**	**48.6**
India (median)	21.5	25.6	48.6

Sources: Data for NER states based on Gross State Domestic Product of NE States (database), North Eastern Development Finance Corporation Ltd., https://databank.nedfi.com/content /gsva-sectoral-contribution-ner; calculation of median based on Handbook of Statistics on the Indian Economy (database), Reserve Bank of India, Mumbai, India, https://www.rbi.org.in/scripts /annualpublications.aspx?head=handbook+of+statistics+on+indian+economy.
Note: Calculations are made using constant 2011–12 prices.

TABLE 2A.4 **Share of employment, 2015–16**
Percent

STATE	PRIMARY	SECONDARY	TERTIARY
Assam	52.0	12.3	35.7
Manipur	40.2	23.8	36.0
Meghalaya	66.9	11.8	21.3
Mizoram	52.9	11.2	35.9
Nagaland	59.6	5.7	34.7
Sikkim	34.0	26.8	39.2
Tripura	26.9	44.0	29.1
Himachal Pradesh	21.0	29.9	49.1
Uttarakhand	38.7	21.6	39.7
India	47.3	22.5	30.2

Source: National Sample Survey Fifth Survey of Employment and Unemployment 2015–16, table 23, http://labourbureaunew.gov.in/UserContent/EUS_5th_1.pdf.
Note: Values are per 1,000 workers ages 15 years and older, by industry, based on National Industrial Classification 2008, https://udyogaadhaar.gov.in/UA/Document/nic_2008_17apr09.pdf, according to the Usual Principal & Subsidiary Status Approach for each state and national territory, rural and urban.

TABLE 2A.5 **Literate population and youth who completed secondary school among all main workers, 2011**

Percent

STATE	LITERATE, 15 YEARS AND OLDER		SECONDARY SCHOOL COMPLETED, YOUTH	
	MALE	FEMALE	MALE	FEMALE
Assam	72.7	52.8	14.3	14.8
Manipur	81.4	61.3	30.0	23.6
Meghalaya	72.2	66.5	11.7	10.7
Mizoram	92.9	88.6	14.3	15.0
Nagaland	79.1	65.1	17.3	12.5
Sikkim	85.4	70.0	18.3	15.4
Tripura	90.6	74.8	16.4	11.8
NER	**75.4**	**58.6**	**15.5**	**14.7**
India	77.8	51.3	25.1	19.7

Source: Census of India 2011, http://www.censusindia.gov.in/DigitalLibrary/Tables.aspx.
Note: Youth are those ages 15–24 years.

TABLE 2A.6 **Labor force participation rate for working-age adults and youth**

Percent

STATE	15 YEARS AND OLDER		YOUTH AGES 15–24	
	MALE	FEMALE	MALE	FEMALE
Assam	86.1	47.2	70.1	46.7
Manipur	81.3	65.9	59.0	54.4
Meghalaya	81.2	60.2	60.0	48.2
Mizoram	81.8	59.9	60.5	48.4
Nagaland	82.5	70.6	61.4	56.3
Sikkim	83.2	60.4	63.2	50.1
Tripura	85.9	59.1	69.1	57.0
NER	**85.0**	**52.2**	**67.4**	**48.7**
India	81.3	43.9	60.6	38.8

Source: Census of India 2011, http://www.censusindia.gov.in/DigitalLibrary/Tables.aspx.

ANNEX 2B: STRUCTURE OF GROSS STATE DOMESTIC PRODUCT

The tertiary sector is the dominant sector, contributing roughly half the gross state domestic product; the share of the primary sector is second, at 30 percent; and the secondary sector constitutes the remaining 20 percent. Although superficially the three focus states appear to have similar shares (figure 2.9, panel a), the underlying subsectors differ in their importance. Assam has a larger mining (petroleum) subsector within the primary sector and a larger share in the manufacturing and trade sectors. Mizoram has negligible manufacturing but more electricity generation and a large public administration service sector. Tripura has more diversified sources of growth in the nonagriculture sectors. The skilled services with trade potential—such as software, accounting, finance, medical, and education—are unfortunately mixed in with professional services and other services in the presentation of the national accounts. More details on shares of GSDP by the originating 11 sectors are presented in table 2B.1.

Of employment, half the share is in the primary sector, except in Tripura (figure 2.9, panel b). The high share of the secondary sector in Tripura is mainly in labor-intensive construction activities. Among services, trade, transport, accommodation and food services, and education seem to dominate. Grouping selected activities as "high-value" skilled services,[21] Mizoram and Sikkim seem to have some edge, with the employment shares slightly above all-India's 7 percent.

TABLE 2B.1 **Share of gross state domestic product, by economic activity, 2014–15**
Percent

ITEM	ASSAM	MANIPUR	MEGHALAYA	MIZORAM	NAGALAND	SIKKIM	TRIPURA	NER
Agriculture, forestry, and fishing	21.2	19.8	19.7	29.6	31.7	7.9	28.6	22.9
Mining and quarrying	8.2	0.0	3.5	0.7	0.5	0.1	5.5	5.7
Primary	**29.4**	**19.8**	**23.2**	**30.3**	**32.2**	**8.0**	**34.1**	**28.6**
Manufacturing	11.6	2.7	16.5	0.6	1.1	41.6	4.9	10.9
Electricity, gas, water supply & other utility services	1.7	2.9	2.7	9.9	1.8	14.4	2.0	3.1
Construction	9.3	11.6	5.5	9.6	6.7	5.3	7.6	8.8
Secondary	**22.6**	**17.2**	**24.7**	**20.2**	**9.6**	**61.2**	**14.5**	**22.8**
Trade, repair, hotels, and restaurants	16.3	13.7	17.6	9.4	7.8	4.8	11.3	13.8
Transport, storage, communication & services related to broadcasting	6.6	6.4	6.2	4.0	4.9	3.2	4.3	5.8
Financial services	3.1	1.9	3.2	2.3	3.9	1.6	3.1	2.9
Real estate, ownership of dwelling & professional services	7.4	8.8	6.5	4.0	9.3	5.0	6.8	6.9
Public administration	6.2	15.3	10.3	15.7	17.7	7.1	12.3	9.0
Other services	8.5	16.8	8.3	14.1	14.7	9.3	13.6	10.2
Tertiary	**48.0**	**62.9**	**52.1**	**49.5**	**58.2**	**30.8**	**51.4**	**48.6**
TOTAL GSVA at basic prices	100	100	100	100	100	100	100	100

Source: Gross State Domestic Product of NE States (database), North Eastern Development Finance Corporation Ltd., https://databank.nedfi.com/content/gsva-sectoral-contribution-ner.
Note: NER = North Eastern Region; GSVA = gross state value added.

NOTES

1. The divergence is noted in Government of India (2017b).
2. The government of India provided a host of incentives to attract industry to NER states through the North East Industrial and Investment Promotion Policy, 2007 (NEIIPP), which has now been replaced by a new incentive package, the North East Industrial Development Scheme, 2017 (Government of India 2018).
3. One-quarter of India's forests are in NER, compared with an 8 percent share of the country's surface area, based on Government of India (2015). Valuation of carbon sequestration is based on World Bank computations, derived from annual use value of forests according to World Bank (2013).
4. In 2000, a city was defined as a population center with 50,000 or more inhabitants. In 2015, a city was defined as a contiguous area with 1,500 or more inhabitants per square kilometer or a majority of built-up land cover coincident with a population center with 50,000 or more inhabitants.
5. Such measures capture the centrality of a node in the context of the whole network, not just as a connection between two points.
6. The census in India defines an area as "urban" when it meets three criteria: (1) a minimum population of 5,000; (2) at least 75 percent of the male working population engaged mainly in nonagricultural pursuits; and (3) a density of population of at least 400 persons per square kilometer. Areas that are declared by statute as towns by local authorities are also counted as urban.
7. The Government of India's Mid-Term Economic Survey 2016–17 used several alternative definitions of population thresholds and the Joint Research Center of the European Commission Science Hub definition, using the Global Human Settlements Layer to elaborate on the measurement issue (Government of India 2017b).
8. "High-density clusters" meet the following criteria: (1) four contiguous cells with at least 1,500 persons per square kilometer; (2) a minimum of 50,000 persons per cluster; and (3) density of built-up area greater than 50 percent.
9. Calculations based on DGCIS (2018).
10. These taxes were documented prior to the introduction of the goods and services tax in 2017.
11. Based on data from Van Leemput (2016).
12. Based on data from Van Leemput (2016, 36).
13. See the area-based exemptions for eligible units in the Himalayas and the NER states: http://www.cbic.gov.in/resources//htdocs-cbec/excise/area-baesd-exemption/Annex-E -GST_Gazette_Nofication-circular.pdf;jsessionid=D70F05EB281915390954E52D0EA FBD3A.
14. Although the official migration statistics infrequently collected from the census and National Sample Surveys lag the current migration trends, the analysis here is confined to official data. The government's 2016–17 Mid-Term Economic Survey innovatively used rail passenger data to suggest that actual interstate migration was nearly twice the estimate from age cohort–based estimates from the censuses of 2001 and 2011 (Government of India 2017). Migration tables from the 2011 census were not available when the Economic Survey was written but have become available and are used here.
15. Fueled by the demographic dividend, the Indian middle class is likely to increase dramatically in the next 20 years. The OECD (2010) estimates that the size of the Indian middle class (measured as household spending between $10 and $100 daily in 2005 purchasing power parity terms) will swell by a billion people by 2039. Using a narrower definition, Ablett et al. (2007) project that the Indian middle class will increase to 600 million, an almost tenfold rise.
16. For details, see the World Health Organization's recommendations at http://www.who.int /mediacentre/factsheets/fs394/en/ (accessed April 10, 2019).
17. Country-specific intakes ranged from 19.2 to 325.1 grams per day for fruits and 34.6 to 493.1 grams per day for vegetables (Micha et al. 2015).
18. Low and Pasadilla (2016) describe in detail the different services involved in the various stages of the manufacturing process: establishment, premanufacture, manufacture, postmanufacture, postsale services, and back-office services, using 22 case studies from around the world.
19. Calculations based on the Annual Survey of Industries, Central Statistics Organization, India.

20. Sophistication is a measure of the average income of states that have specialized in these products (Hausmann, Hwang, and Rodrik 2007).
21. "High-value skilled services" include activities in information and communication, finance and insurance, administration and support services, human health, and social work. Other service activities are those grouped as "high-value services."

REFERENCES

Ablett, J., A. Baijal, E. Beinhocker, A. Bose, D. Farrell, U. Gersch, E. Greenberg, S. Gupta, and S. Gupta. 2007. "The 'Bird of Gold': The Rise of India's Consumer Market." McKinsey Global Institute, New York. https://www.mckinsey.com/featured-insights/asia-pacific/the-bird-of-gold.

DGCIS (Directorate General of Commercial Intelligence Statistics). 2018. *Monthly Bulletin of Foreign Trade Statistics* (April). Kolkata: DGCIS.

FICCI (Federation of Indian Chambers of Commerce and Industry). 2018. *Taxpayers' Goods and Services Tax Implementation Experience Survey, 2018*. http://ficci.in/Sedocument/20429/FICCI-Industry-survey-report-on-GST.pdf.

Government of India. 2014. *Report of the Expert Group to Review Methodology for Measurement of Poverty*. New Delhi: Planning Commission, Government of India.

——. 2015. *State of Forest Report, 2015*. New Delhi: Forest Survey of India, Ministry of Environment, Forest and Climate Change, Government of India.

——. 2017a. *Agricultural Statistics at a Glance 2016*. New Delhi: Ministry of Agriculture and Farmers Welfare, Government of India. http://eands.dacnet.nic.in/PDF/Glance-2016.pdf.

——. 2017b. *Economic Survey 2016–17*. New Delhi: Ministry of Finance, Government of India. https://www.indiabudget.gov.in/budget2017-2018/e_survey2.asp.

——. 2018. The Gazette of India, April 13, 2018, REGD. NO. D.L.-33004/99. New Delhi: Ministry of Commerce and Industry, Government of India.

Hallward-Driemier, M., and G. Nayyar. 2018. *Trouble in the Making: The Future of Manufacturing-Led Development*. Washington, DC: World Bank.

Hausmann, R., J. Hwang, and D. Rodrik. 2007. "What You Export Matters." *Journal of Economic Growth* 12 (1): 1–25.

Huria, S., R. Manghnani, S. Saez, and E. van der Marel. Forthcoming. "Servicification of Indian Manufacturing." World Bank, Washington, DC.

Lanz, R., and A. Maurer. 2015. "Services and Global Value Chains: Some Evidence on Servicification of Manufacturing and Services Networks." Working Paper ERSD-2015-03, World Trade Organization, Geneva.

Low, P., and G. O. Pasadilla. 2016. "Manufacturing-Related Services." In *Services in Global Value Chains: Manufacturing-Related Services*, 1–58. Singapore: APEC Policy Support Unit, Asia-Pacific Economic Cooperation.

Micha, R., S. Khatibzadeh, P. Shi, K. G. Andrews, R. E. Engell, and D. Mozaffarian. 2015. "Global, Regional and National Consumption of Major Food Groups in 1990 and 2010: A Systematic Analysis Including 266 Country-Specific Nutrition Surveys Worldwide." BMJ Open, e008705. doi:10.1136/bmjopen-2015- 008705.

MORTH (Ministry of Road Transport and Highways). 2017. *GST Is Good and Simple Tax*. New Delhi: MORTH. http://pibphoto.nic.in/documents/rlink/2017/jul/p201772601.pdf.

Mukherjee, S., D. Chakraborty, and S. Sikdar. 2014. "Three Decades of Human Development across the Indian States: Inclusive Growth or Perpetual Disparity?" Working Paper No. 2014-139, National Institute of Public Policy, New Delhi.

NSSO (National Sample Survey Office). 2008. "Migration in India: July 2007–June 2008." Report No. 533, NSSO, Ministry of Statistics and Programme Implementation, Government of India, New Delhi.

OECD (Organisation for Economic Co-operation and Development). 2010. "The Emerging Middle Class in Developing Countries." Working Paper No. 285, OECD, Paris. https://www.oecd.org/dev/44457738.pdf.

Roy, A., N. U. Singh, D. S. Dkhar, A. K. Mohanty, S. B. Singh, and A. K. Tripathi. 2016. "Food Security in North-East Region of India: A State-Wise Analysis." *Agricultural Economics Research Review* 28 (Conf. No.): 259–66.

UNICEF (United Nations Children's Fund). 2012. "Policy Brief: For a Better Inclusion of Internal Migrants in India." UNICEF, New York.

Van Leemput, E. 2016. "A Passage to India: Quantifying Internal and External Barriers to Trade." International Finance Discussion Paper 1185, Federal Reserve Board of Governors, Washington, DC. https://doi.org/10.17016/IFDP.2016.1185.

Van Leemput, E., and E. A. Wiencek. 2017. "The Effect of the GST on Indian Growth." International Finance Discussion Paper, Federal Reserve Board of Governors, Washington, DC. https://doi.org/10.17016/2573-2129.29.

Weiss, D. J., A. Nelson, H. S. Gibson, W. Temperley, S. Peedell, A. Lieber, M. Hancher, et al. 2018. "A Global Map of Travel Time to Cities to Assess Inequalities in Accessibility in 2015." *Nature* 553 (January 18): 333–36.

World Bank. 2013. "Diagnostic Assessment of Environmental Challenges." Report IN-700004, World Bank, Washington, DC.

3 Connectivity Assessment
CHALLENGES AND OPPORTUNITIES

PRABIR DE AND CHARLES KUNAKA

STRATEGIC CONTEXT

The North Eastern Region (NER) of India is connected to the rest of India through, the Siliguri Corridor, a narrow tract of land only 27 kilometers (km) wide, commonly known as the "Chicken's Neck." International borders account for 98 percent of the region's perimeter, with China and Bhutan to the north, Myanmar to the east, Bangladesh to the south and west, and Nepal to the west (Government of India 2008, 5). Trade has always held special significance for the economies of NER states. Indeed, with its abundant natural resources and strong connectivity with the rest of India and the world, NER flourished as a trade and commerce hub at the turn of the 20th century. Global trade was conducted through the Port of Chittagong in present-day Bangladesh and the Port of Kolkata in present-day India, which were connected to the region through the network of inland waterways provided by the Brahmaputra-Barak River Systems and their tributaries, as well as by roads and railways. The railway line from Dibrugarh (in Assam, present-day India) to Chittagong (in present-day Bangladesh) was one of the first railway lines in Asia.

The path of NER's growth and development changed with the division of the Indian subcontinent, first in 1947, with the split of colonial India into India, West Pakistan, and East Pakistan, and then in 1971, with the separation of East Pakistan from West Pakistan and the creation of Bangladesh. This division interrupted inland water, road, and railway connections through Bangladesh and meant the loss of access to the Port of Chittagong, the gateway to East Asia and Southeast Asia. The loss of connectivity contributed to the region's falling behind the rest of the country in the pace of economic growth and development.

There are three scales on which connectivity in NER can be analyzed—within NER, between NER and the rest of India, and between NER and neighboring countries. First, overall, trade and transport connectivity within NER is dominated by the distribution of goods and services that are sourced mostly from the rest of India. Assam is the main hub for the distribution of goods in NER and the central node in the connectivity map of the region. Second, the main trade and traffic exchanges between NER and the rest of India take place along a route that passes through the Siliguri Corridor. Estimates show that more than 40 million tonnes of goods flow through the "Chicken's Neck" (e.g., Government of Bangladesh 2011). Road transport predominates, followed by rail. Inland waterways transport (IWT), transiting through Bangladesh, carries very small volumes of traffic. Third, there are bilateral trade flows between NER and neighboring countries. In 2015–16, imports and exports worth $84 million and $230 million, respectively, were traded between NER and Bangladesh. Most of the trade moves by road, transloading at the border from trucks of one country to those of the other. There are also some shipments that move by train and waterways, but these are still a small proportion of the overall traffic. Trade flows between NER and Myanmar and through it to the wider Association of Southeast Asian Nations (ASEAN) region and China consist of localized flows of agricultural products from Myanmar and manufactured products from NER states along the border.

The regional economy in NER is dominated by the tertiary and primary sectors, which account for almost 50 percent and 30 percent, respectively, of real gross state domestic product (GSDP); the secondary sector accounts for a smaller share of about 20 percent (see chapter 2). The industries in NER states include coke and refined petroleum products; food products; and a range of manufactured products, including wood, furniture, beverages, medicinal chemical and botanical products, metal products, and rubber and plastic products. The manufacturing activities are based on locally available resources.[1]

Transport and logistics bottlenecks have long been identified as serious constraints to the industrial growth of NER (e.g., De 2011; Sarma and Bezbaruah 2009; Brunner 2010; and Das and Thomas 2016). Improvement of transportation networks would help unlock NER's growth potential, especially given its geographical proximity to the growing Southeast Asian and East Asian markets. For instance, although trade between India and Myanmar has increased sharply in the past one and a half decades, the trade volume remains below potential. A significant proportion of NER's cross-border trade with Myanmar is transit trade from China, most of which consists of smuggled goods (e.g., RIS 2012; De and Ray 2013).

This chapter focuses on trade and transport connectivity in NER and especially between NER and its neighboring economies. Although this study does not go into detail on services, trade in services, such as tourism and the associated movement of people, places additional demands on connectivity. The rest of the chapter is organized as follows. The next section outlines the connectivity of NER, followed by a discussion of the economic links between NER and neighboring countries. The chapter then discusses the physical network connectivity between NER and neighboring countries. The last section presents the main findings of the analysis and proposes recommendations to enhance the connectivity of NER.

THE CONNECTIVITY OF NER

Road connectivity

Road transport is the dominant mode of transport in NER. The region has a road network of about 145,000 km, comprising 35,000 km of surfaced roads and 110,000 km of unsurfaced roads (ADB 2011). Of the surfaced roads,

8,480 km are national highways (table 3.1) and the rest are state highways and district roads, some of which are at the national highway standard. However, although the length of roads per capita may be relatively high—for instance, more than 3,000 km per 1,000 square km of area in Tripura (KPMG 2015)—the quality of the roads in the region is poor, with many substandard timber bridges (particularly in Assam, Sikkim, and Tripura) that require restrictions on axle loads. Reasons for the low density and poor quality of road infrastructure include the hilly terrain and low population density that characterize much of NER. These two factors increase the costs of road building while reducing the viability of high-cost, high-quality roads. The problems with the road network are compounded by poor maintenance. Several of the states have limited budgets for maintenance, and efforts to expand the networks stretch resources even further. Thus, many of the roads are in a state of disrepair.

The government has been pursuing a large-scale program to develop road infrastructure in NER. The North Eastern Region Vision 2020 and the 11th Five-Year Plan emphasize the importance of expanding and improving maintenance of the road network at all levels, from village tracks to the national highway network. Investments are being made to upgrade the state highways into national highways, with emphasis on connecting district headquarter towns in NER, under the Special Accelerated Road Development Programme for the North Eastern Region (SARDP-NE).[2] The central master plan for road connectivity in the region aims to upgrade all national highways to four lanes and connect all state capitals and subdivisional headquarters by all-weather roads.

To improve NER's connectivity with the rest of India, corridors have been defined and road connectivity is being improved. One of the major corridors is the East-West Corridor, which connects Srirampur on the West Bengal–Assam border and extends to Silchar in Assam.[3] The 670-km stretch of the East-West Corridor between Srirampur and Silchar is being converted into a four-lane highway.

TABLE 3.1 **Distribution of national highways in NER by state**
Kilometers

STATE	LENGTH OF NATIONAL HIGHWAYS
Assam	2,836
Manipur	959
Meghalaya	810
Mizoram	927
Nagaland	494
Sikkim	62
Tripura	400
NER	8,480

Source: World Bank compilation of data from the Ministry of Development of North Eastern Region (MDoNER).
Note: NER = North Eastern Region.

Railway connectivity

The ongoing expansion of rail connectivity in NER is of great potential importance. The network expansion offers the prospect of high-speed rail connectivity between the Chinese city of Kunming in Yunnan province and Kolkata in India through Mandalay in Myanmar and Dhaka in Bangladesh. Ultimately, the wider network will connect NER to a collective market of close to half a billion people. However, improving rail connectivity faces many challenges and will take time; the existing railways are unreliable and have been losing traffic. In addition, the network is made up of a mixture of narrow- and broad-gauge systems with several interchange points for bilateral traffic. Nevertheless, the government of India has been implementing an aggressive program to develop the railway network in NER.

The present rail network in NER comprises about 4,136 km of route length, mostly broad gauge (BG) (table 3.2). All the states in the region are included in the development plans of the BG network, and indeed they are already connected to the BG map of the country. The capital of Tripura (Agartala) is connected with a BG line, and the capital of Manipur will be connected with a BG line by 2020. As many as 29 new trains were introduced in the region in 2016 and 2017.

There are several ongoing railway network improvement projects in NER to form integral links of the Northeast Frontier Railway network. Some of the significant projects that have been completed in recent years are the Guwahati-Tinsukia-Dibrugarh, including the Furkating-Jorhat-Mariani and Simaluguri-Sibsagar-Moranhat branch lines in Assam. Another BG line between Dudhnoi (Assam) and Mendhipathar (Meghalaya) was completed, linking Meghalaya to the BG railway network. Construction of a new 26-km BG railway line from Mukongselek (Assam) to Pasighat is ongoing. The combined rail and road Bogibeel Bridge, which connects the North Bank of the Brahmaputra River with the South Bank at Dibrugarh in Upper Assam, was inaugurated in December 2018. Mizoram was connected to the Indian Railway network

TABLE 3.2 Railway route length in NER by state

Kilometers

STATE	ROUTE LENGTH			
	BROAD GAUGE	METER GAUGE	NARROW GAUGE	TOTAL
Assam	2,464.89	0.00	0.00	2,464.89
Manipur	12.56	0.00	0.00	12.56
Meghalaya	8.76	0.00	0.00	8.76
Mizoram	1.50	0.00	0.00	1.50
Nagaland	11.13	0.00	0.00	11.13
Tripura	215.86	0.00	0.00	215.86
Bihar	327.26	0.34	0.00	327.60
West Bengal	994.68	0.00	87.48	1,082.16
NER	4,048.31	0.34	87.48	4,136.13

Source: Northeast Frontier Railway 2018.
Note: Values are as of April 27, 2018. Parts of Bihar and West Bengal are covered under the Northeast Frontier Railway. NER = North Eastern Region.

in November 2014, when a 54-km line from Kathahal (Assam) to Bhairabi (Mizoram) was inaugurated. Since May 2016, a passenger train has been shuttling between Bhairabi and Silchar (Assam) through Kathahal.

Ongoing railway network extension projects include the following:

- Tripura: A 15-km stretch between Agartala and Akhaura in Bangladesh, which, once completed, will substantially reduce the rail distance between Agartala and Kolkata, from the present 1,590 km to 499 km, and a 114-km BG line from Silchar in Assam to Agartala in Tripura and thereafter to the border town of Sabroom, also in Tripura, from which the Port of Chittagong in Bangladesh is only 75 km.
- Manipur: Work is presently ongoing on the 84-km Jiribam-Tupul section of the railway and is likely to be completed by 2020. Thereafter, the railway line will be extended to Imphal, the capital of Manipur.
- Mizoram: Work is ongoing and scheduled to be completed by 2020 on a line from Bhairabi to Sairang, 20 km from Aizawl.
- Meghalaya: Preparatory work on a 108-km stretch of the proposed Byrnihat-Shillong railway project has been completed.
- Nagaland: Work on an 83-km rail link between Dhansiri in Assam and Zubza, near Nagaland's capital, Kohima, is ongoing. However, delays in land acquisition in Assam have held up progress on the first phase of the project—Dhansiri to Sukhovi (16 km)—which was scheduled to be completed by 2019.
- Sikkim: The 52-km BG railway between Sevoke (West Bengal) and Rangpo (Sikkim) has been delayed by a variety of factors, including land acquisition, environmental concerns, and security issues.

There is no railway link between India and Bhutan at present. However, the government of India has identified five potential rail links: (1) a 57-km line from Kokhrajhar (Assam) to Gelephu (Bhutan); (2) a 51.15-km line from Pathsala (Assam) to Nanglam (Bhutan); (3) a 48-km line from Rangiya (Assam) to Samdrupjongkjar (Bhutan); (4) a 23-km line from Banarhat (West Bengal) to Samtse (Bhutan); and (5) a 17.52-km line from Hasimara (West Bengal) to Phuentsholing (Bhutan).

Between India and Nepal, there are two railway lines in operation: Raxaul-Sirsiya and Jaynagar-Janakpur. The former is a line of approximately 6 km from Raxaul (India) to Sirsiya Inland Container Depot, located near Birgunj (Nepal). The latter is a 53-km line from Jaynagar (India) to Janakpur (Nepal). India and Nepal have plans to connect by rail New Jalpaiguri (India) to Kakarbhitta (Nepal); Jogbani (India) to Biratnagar (Nepal); Nautanwa (India) to Bhairahawa (Nepal); and Nepalganj Road (India) to Nepalganj (Nepal).

Significant developments in railway connectivity that are expected by 2020 include (1) the connection of Imphal (Manipur) to the BG railway network; (2) a link between Agartala (Tripura) and Kolkata (West Bengal) through Bangladesh; (3) the connection of Guwahati (Assam), Silchar (Assam), and Agartala (Tripura) with the Port of Chittagong (Bangladesh); and (4) BG links to all the state capitals in NER. Other regional connectivity projects include the resumption of railway line construction between Imphal (Manipur) and Moreh (Manipur), on the India-Myanmar border; extension of Indian railway lines into Nepal, at various points in addition to Birgunj, which is already connected; and connection of Bhutan and India by railway.

Inland waterways connectivity

IWT has great potential for significant cost savings in transportation in NER.[4] NER has about 1,800 km of river routes that can be used by steamers and larger country boats (MDoNER 2019). The Brahmaputra and Barak Rivers have long been used for transportation.[5] Since 1988, the stretch along the Brahmaputra River from Sadiya to Dhubri (891 km) in Assam has been declared National Waterway 2 (NW-2). However, only shallow draft barges can move along NW-2, due to low navigability. In addition, night operations are not possible in some places along the river. Night navigation aids have recently been installed, however, on the 440-km stretch between Dhubri (on the Bangladesh-India border) and Silghat.[6] Differential Global Positioning Systems stations were set up at Dibrugarh, Silghat, Jogighopa, and Dhubri. The stations promote safe navigation using electronic charts.

Ongoing investments in the waterways should help strengthen cross-border connectivity, particularly with Bangladesh. A 121-km stretch of the Barak River from Lakhipur (Assam) to Bhanga (Assam) on the India-Bangladesh border has been declared National Waterway 6 and is being improved, mainly through dredging of the fairway. In addition, improvements are being made to the terminals at Badarpur (Assam) and Karimganj (Assam), and a new floating terminal is being built at Silchar (Assam).[7]

At the regional level, IWT services between India and Bangladesh are governed by the Protocol on Inland Water Transit and Trade (PIWTT), which allows movement of cargo from Haldia-Kolkata (West Bengal) to Karimganj-Guwahati (Assam) in NER and back through Bangladesh. PIWTT was recently renewed to run until March 31, 2020, and has a provision for automatic renewal. Poor infrastructure, especially terminals, has long hampered the efficient handling of cargo. However, improvements are under way in Bangladesh and India to improve several IWT terminals, including the Ashuganj river terminal in Bangladesh. Ashuganj has road links and customs facilities for transit cargo to NER through the Akhaura (Bangladesh)–Agartala (Tripura, India) land border and links to the Port of Chittagong.

To enhance inland and coastal waterway connectivity between the two countries for trade and cruise movements, India and Bangladesh signed several other agreements in 2018, among them: (1) an agreement to use the Chattogram (Chittagong) and Mongla ports in Bangladesh for movement of goods to and from India; (2) a standard operating procedure for movement of passenger and cruise vessels on the inland protocol route and coastal shipping routes; and (3) an addendum to the PIWTT between India and Bangladesh for inclusion of Dhubri in India and Pangaon in Bangladesh as new ports of call.[8] These initiatives are complemented by the India-Bangladesh Coastal Shipping Agreement, which was signed in June 2015. The agreement provides for direct connectivity between seaports in East India and Bangladesh. Taken together, these initiatives provide a much more flexible system for transport and logistics that can only benefit NER.

Easing of navigation through NW-2 promises substantial gains in terms of commercial and environmental costs. Cargo transportation through NW-2 has been rising, albeit slowly (table 3.3). Exports to Bangladesh using IWT have also increased in recent years.

Currently, the major cargoes transported through NW-2 comprise food grains, electricity generation and transmission equipment, fertilizers, building materials, and bamboo. However, the potential for transporting

TABLE 3.3 **Cargo transportation through NW-2**
Million tonnes

YEAR	WITHIN NW-2	TRANSPORTED TO NER FROM KOLKATA	EXPORTS TO BANGLADESH FROM KOLKATA
2008–09	2.18	0.00	0.88
2009–10	2.11	0.00	1.34
2010–11	2.16	0.00	1.49
2011–12	2.41	0.02	0.15
2012–13	2.43	0.02	1.68
2013–14	2.45	0.01	1.87
2014–15	2.51	0.01	2.01
2015–16	2.58	0.02	2.43

Source: Inland Waterways Authority of India.
Note: A major portion of the cargo in NW-2 is being transported through ferry service, for distances up to 100 kilometers. NER = North Eastern Region; NW-2 = National Waterway 2.

project-based cargo over this route is high because of planned hydro and thermal power plants in NER. The plants include 34 hydroelectric projects for which memorandums of understanding have been signed. The construction of these hydro projects would require about 24 million tonnes of cement and 2 million tonnes of steel through 2026. In general, waterways can easily handle overdimensional cargo (cargo that protrudes outside the loading deck of the vehicle or barge). The Inland Waterways Authority of India (IWAI) has already signed a memorandum of understanding with Indian private sector companies, including Jindal Steel and Power and Reliance Power.

A joint study by Inland Waterways Authority of India (IWAI) and Rail India Technical and Economic Service (RITES) estimates that there will be significant movement of cargo by 2031–32 at Jogighopa (10.03 million tonnes, consisting mostly of coal) and Pandu (14.63 million tonnes, consisting of food items, cement, coal, fertilizers, and building materials) (IWAI and RITES 2014).

Furthermore, a considerable volume of commercial goods is already being transported across shorter stretches along the NW-2 in Assam, which is dominated mainly by the unorganized sector. For instance, in Lower Assam, which is marked by several small islands, day-to-day necessities are transported by the unorganized sector for the stretches between Dhubri and Hatsinghimari and Phulbari near Meghalaya. Promoting the use of waterways can lead to greater economic activity in communities along the riverbanks, which in turn will have a positive impact on local economies and livelihoods.

Air connectivity

As with other modes of transport, NER accounts for only a minuscule proportion (less than 1 percent) of all traffic handled by the top airports in India. In addition to Guwahati in Assam, only Agartala (Tripura) and Imphal (Manipur) in NER are placed among the top 50 airports in the country. The terrain of NER makes overland transport costly and unreliable, increasing the need for air transport connectivity. Air transport plays an important role in sustaining commerce, tourism, and the realization of the potential of high-value horticulture and floriculture in the region. However, the same terrain that hampers land transport also affects air transport by increasing the cost of building airports.

Due to thin population densities and the high cost of providing infrastructure, air transport in NER has in the past been supported by subsidies. State governments provide some helicopter services at subsidized rates, especially in Sikkim, Tripura, Nagaland, and Meghalaya. However, the introduction of smaller and more efficient aircraft has enabled the expansion of air transport services. Within NER, Guwahati is the preeminent hub; Drukair, Royal Bhutan Airlines, connects Guwahati to Paro (Bhutan) and Bangkok (Thailand). Often there is no direct connectivity between other state capitals except through Guwahati. In some cases, travel from one state to another goes through Kolkata, which is the main gateway to the rest of India and the outside world.

All the states are connected by air, although some, like Meghalaya and Sikkim, have no airports that can handle wide-body aircraft. Several facilities are under development across the region. The Sixth Sectoral Summit of the North Eastern Council on Air Connectivity set a target of "operationalizing up to 50 airports/airstrips in the North Eastern Region by the end of the 11th Five-Year Plan, and providing up to 600 flights per week within the region, by using the appropriate type of aircraft, making the required improvements in existing airports/airstrips in a time-bound manner" (Government of India 2007). A new airport at Pakyong (Sikkim) opened in September 2018 as the first greenfield airport in NER; some other projects are under way. The facilities at existing airports also need to be improved. Among the operational airports, only Agartala and Guwahati have night landing facilities, and Instrument Landing Systems (ILS)[9] are available only in Agartala, Dibrugarh, Dimapur, Guwahati, and Imphal.

Air connectivity in NER is needed to support some of the region's key sectors for potential development, especially high-value agriculture and services. Air transport is important for moving perishable commodities, developing tourism, developing centers such as Shillong as educational hubs, and providing resilience for the transport networks in the event of disruptions to the land transport systems. The potential to harness regional markets has yet to be fully exploited. Direct connectivity could be enhanced with neighboring countries and ASEAN economies. Presently, there are only limited international flights from Guwahati, which is the only designated international airport. There are no air links with Myanmar or Bangladesh from the region; travel to either country requires connections through Kolkata or Bangkok.

The government of Assam has been trying to develop air connectivity between Guwahati and neighboring countries under the Ministry of Civil Aviation's regional airport development plan, known as Ude Desh ka Aam Naagrik (UDAN) 3. Flights were launched in 2018 between Guwahati and Dhaka, Guwahati and Bangkok, and Guwahati and Hong Kong SAR, China.

ECONOMIC LINKS BETWEEN NER AND NEIGHBORING ECONOMIES

Trade-related demand for connectivity in NER can arise not only from its own trade with the rest of India and its immediate neighbors, but also from potential transit trade between Bangladesh, Bhutan, India, and Nepal (BBIN) and ASEAN.

Potential demands for transit trade are growing, although as of 2018 most of such trade did not go through NER. Although ASEAN's exports to BBIN increased from $120.63 billion in 2012 to $150.60 billion in 2016, ASEAN's imports from BBIN decreased from $57.66 billion in 2012 to $44.20 billion in 2016.[10] ASEAN's market access to BBIN has increased, although marginally—over 3.3 percent of ASEAN's global exports in 2016 went to BBIN, compared with 2.8 percent in 2012.

Trade between BBIN and ASEAN is mostly driven by India. Over 90 percent of ASEAN's imports from BBIN have been contributed by India alone, while over 76 percent of ASEAN's exports have been to India.[11] India's exports to ASEAN are primarily petroleum products, bovine meat, and cotton yarn, whereas India's major imports from ASEAN are relatively diversified, including telecom products, electronics, automobile parts and components, edible oil, coal, and petroleum oils.[12] India and ASEAN implemented a free trade area in goods in January 2010. The free trade area has considerably reduced tariffs for almost 80 percent of the products, but due to stringent and complex nontariff measures, some of the sectors and products are denied market access in ASEAN and India.[13] Thus, streamlining of nontariff measures is important for facilitating preferential market access between ASEAN and India and can provide further impetus to bilateral trade.

Meanwhile, trade between NER and two of its largest immediate neighbors, Myanmar and Bangladesh, is growing and generating increased demands for improvements in connectivity.

NER's trade with Myanmar

NER's trade with Myanmar is conducted almost entirely over land routes. Formal trade takes place through various land customs stations (LCSs). All four NER states bordering Myanmar have operational LCSs, including Moreh (Manipur, India)–Tamu (Myanmar); Zokhawthar-Champai (Mizoram, India)–Rih (Myanmar);[14] and Avangkhu (Nagaland, India)–Somara (Myanmar), which has been bilaterally agreed on between the two countries, but has yet to be officially notified (De and Ray 2013). Moreh (Manipur) has been the most significant in volume of trade, followed by Zokhawthar-Champai (Mizoram).

Historically, NER's trade with Myanmar was restricted. However, starting in 1995, border trade was permitted in notified products only,[15] to facilitate the exchange of locally produced commodities along the Indo-Myanmar border. Over time, that list was increased to include 62 tradable products. Border trade was upgraded to normal most-favored-nation trade at Moreh, effective December 1, 2015.[16] Trade facilitation has also seen an improvement through various measures, including setting up a food-testing laboratory in Imphal (Manipur). The government of Myanmar has allowed entry of travelers from third countries through all land border posts with India.

NER's trade with Myanmar has been growing rapidly in recent years. NER's exports to Myanmar through the land border increased from $4.50 million in 2010–11 to $18.62 million in 2015–16, while its imports increased from $8.30 million to $53.02 million over the same years (table 3.4). Total trade with Myanmar stands at $71.64 million, with NER's imports from Myanmar almost three times greater than its exports in 2015–16. Further, NER's informal trade with Myanmar is estimated to be greater than its formal trade (e.g., RIS 2012).

TABLE 3.4 **Trends in NER's trade with Myanmar**
$, millions

YEAR	NER'S EXPORTS TO MYANMAR	NER'S IMPORTS FROM MYANMAR	NER'S TOTAL TRADE WITH MYANMAR
2010–11	4.50	8.30	12.80
2011–12	6.54	8.87	15.41
2012–13	11.67	26.96	38.63
2013–14	17.71	30.92	48.63
2014–15	18.11	42.61	60.72
2015–16	18.62	53.02	71.64

Sources: World Bank estimates from various sources.
Note: Although the data do not allow disaggregation, most of the trade through NER LCSs with Myanmar is assumed to be NER-Myanmar trade, because trade through overland routes linking NER to China, Myanmar, and Bangladesh tends to be localized. The statistics on India-Myanmar border trade differ across sources. Trade data capture exports and imports through border trade for the period preceding December 1, 2015, the date on which India-Myanmar border trade was upgraded to normal most-favored-nation trade. NER = North Eastern Region; LCS = land custom station.

TABLE 3.5 **NER's trade with Myanmar, 2015–16**

NAME OF LCS	MAJOR COMMODITIES TRADED (FORMAL TRADE)	
	EXPORTS	IMPORTS
Moreh (Manipur)	Cumin seed, cotton yarn, auto parts, soya bean meal, wheat flour, and pharmaceuticals	Betel nuts, dry ginger, green mung beans, black matpe beans, turmeric roots, resin, and medicinal herbs
Zokhawthar (Mizoram)	..	Betel nuts

Source: World Bank estimates based on data from Indian Customs.
Note: .. = negligible; NER = North Eastern Region; LCS = land customs station.

NER's exports to Myanmar, which take place largely through the Moreh-Tamu land border, comprise mainly manufactured products, while imports are largely agricultural products (table 3.5). However, in addition to the recorded trade flows, there is anecdotal evidence of the prevalence of smuggling of items such as fertilizers; vehicles, particularly two-wheelers; and other items from India to Myanmar through the land border (e.g., De and Ray 2013). The formal trade volume at Moreh appears to be less than the informal trade volume. Services trade between NER and Myanmar has been growing in tourism, health, hospitality, and education.

The border infrastructure is inadequate and unlikely to support the rising trade volumes between NER and Myanmar. Moreh-Tamu suffers not only from a lack of the hardware and software of modern trade infrastructure, but also from the absence of adequate security, thus making the entire trading environment uncertain. Border infrastructure through India's ambitious Integrated Check Post project at Moreh was inaugurated in January 2019. However, conducting trade through the Integrated Check Post may remain problematic, because connectivity on both sides of the India-Myanmar border remains underdeveloped. For trade flows between the two countries to grow faster, improvements will be required in connectivity through the land border as well as in the border infrastructure, at international standards, at all the LCSs on both sides of the India-Myanmar border.

NER's trade with Bangladesh

Currently, NER has 26 LCSs with Bangladesh, of which 20 are functional (table 3.6). Assam, Tripura and Meghalaya are the only states with functional LCSs. Mizoram has 1 designated LCS, but it is not functional.

NER contributes only 4 percent of India's exports to Bangladesh. The total trade between NER and Bangladesh doubled, to reach $313.27 million in 2015–16, from $156.07 million in 2010–11. At the national level, India and NER have a trade surplus with Bangladesh. In recent years, NER's trade surplus with Bangladesh has risen, as NER's exports have increased at a faster pace than its imports (see table 3.7).

As indicated in annex 3A, which presents the top five traded products by LCS, NER's exports to Bangladesh are mostly primary products, such as horticultural products and minerals. They comprise coal, quick lime, ginger, oranges and other citrus fruits, boulder stones, dry fish, raw hides, and woven fabrics and synthetic filament. In contrast, NER's imports from Bangladesh are diversified and mostly secondary items, such as cement, processed foods, plastics, knitted and crocheted synthetic fabrics, garments, fish, PVC pipe, and wooden furniture.

TABLE 3.6 **Trading with Bangladesh: Number of LCSs**

NER STATE	FUNCTIONAL	NONFUNCTIONAL	TOTAL
Assam	5	3	8
Meghalaya	8	2	10
Mizoram	0	1	1
Tripura	7	0	7
Total	20	6	26

Source: De 2011.
Note: LCSs = land customs stations; NER = North Eastern Region.

TABLE 3.7 **Trends in NER's trade with Bangladesh**
$, millions

YEAR	NER'S EXPORTS TO BANGLADESH (% OF TOTAL INDIA EXPORTS)	INDIA'S EXPORTS TO BANGLADESH	NER'S IMPORTS FROM BANGLADESH (% OF TOTAL INDIA IMPORTS)	INDIA'S IMPORTS FROM BANGLADESH	NER'S TOTAL TRADE WITH BANGLADESH (% OF TOTAL TRADE)	INDIA'S TOTAL TRADE WITH BANGLADESH
2010–11	91.6 (2.8)	3,242.9	64.5 (14.4)	446.8	156.1 (4.2)	3,689.7
2011–12	134.6 (3.6)	3,789.2	81.9 (14.0)	585.7	216.6 (5.0)	4,374.9
2012–13	171.2 (3.3)	5,145.0	75.8 (11.9)	639.3	247.0 (4.3)	5,784.3
2013–14	172.7 (2.8)	6,166.9	80.9 (16.7)	484.3	253.6 (3.8)	6,651.3
2014–15	221.3 (3.4)	6,451.5	85.5 (13.8)	621.4	306.8 (4.3)	7,072.8
2015–16	229.4 (3.8)	6,034.9	83.9 (11.5)	727.2	313.3 (4.6)	6,762.1

Sources: World Bank calculations based on Export-Import Databank for India-Bangladesh trade and Indian Customs for NER-Bangladesh trade.

PHYSICAL CONNECTIVITY BETWEEN NER AND NEIGHBORING ECONOMIES

Given its strategic location as the hinge between South Asia and Southeast Asia, NER faces several challenges in transportation connectivity, affecting all modes of transport. Some problems, such as those facing railway transport, are severe and can be overcome only through high levels of investment; while others, especially those relating to road and water transport, are surmountable even in the short term. A proven way to tackle problems along international corridors is to consider the key constraints that are faced on each.

Trade between South Asia and East Asia has traditionally been through maritime connectivity. The Port of Colombo (Sri Lanka) is the region's primary container transshipment port. It had the largest share of India's foreign transshipment volume in 2018, accounting for 42 percent of container traffic (Drewry and Gateway Research 2018). The Colombo container terminal has feeder connections to Indian ports on the east and west coasts. However, traffic between these Indian ports and NER is carried by overland transport services. The road and rail corridors connecting NER to the rest of India and neighboring economies are therefore very important. In addition, the opening of Myanmar has created an opportunity for overland connectivity between the NER and ASEAN regions, especially through Myanmar's Sittwe Port. Transport corridor investments can be transformational and pave the way for greater economic and social welfare in NER. But they need to be designed to enhance and spread the gains while reducing the probability of negative outcomes (e.g., ADB et al. 2018). This section discusses some of the important projects connecting NER with neighboring economies.

Trilateral Corridor (India-Myanmar-Thailand)

The Trilateral Corridor is based on an agreement between India, Myanmar, and Thailand to improve connectivity among them. It is approximately 1,360 km long and integrates Asian Highways 1 and 2. The agreed-on route of the corridor is Moreh (India)–Tamu (Myanmar)–Kalewa-Yargi-Monywa-Mandalay-NayPyiTaw-Yangon-Thaton-Hypaan-Kawkareik-Myawaddy (Myanmar)–Mae Sot (Thailand).

This corridor still suffers from poor infrastructure connectivity. It comprises roads and bridges whose conditions vary, ranging from poor to good. The roads are mostly narrow, winding, and prone to landslides, especially in India. In Myanmar, the corridor consists of national road AH1, sections of which are in very poor condition. Many of the bridges are not engineered to carry heavy vehicle loads. Although some of the bridges along the corridor have been upgraded by the Indian government, others remain in poor condition, with weight restrictions of only 13 tonnes. At the main border stations of Zokhawtar-Rih and Moreh-Tamu, the bridges are very narrow, even for existing traffic. The roads approaching these border posts are narrow, poorly maintained, and often congested with motorized and nonmotorized traffic.

Under the Trilateral Corridor project, various works to improve infrastructure are being implemented. India is responsible for building 78 km of road links, upgrading 58 km of existing roads, improving a further 132 km of roads in Myanmar, and replacing 69 old bridges on the Tamu-Kalewa Friendship Road.

In addition to infrastructure upgrades, the availability and quality of road transport services must be improved. A Trilateral Motor Vehicle Agreement is being negotiated. The agreement will allow cargo and passenger vehicles to move seamlessly along the Trilateral Corridor. The trade that flows through this corridor, or some part thereof, passes through two major border crossing points between India and Myanmar, Moreh (India)–Tamu (Myanmar) and Zokhawthar (India)–Rih (Myanmar).[17]

Moreh-Tamu

The Moreh-Tamu border post is the major border crossing between India and Myanmar, handling the largest volume of traffic. The nearest large town or city in India is Imphal (Manipur), through which there is a link to Guwahati (Assam), which is the main gateway to the NER states. Moreh LCS has been upgraded to an Integrated Check Post and has been fully operational since January 2019. However, the LCS at Tamu has been suffering from capacity constraints. Cross-border traffic through the Moreh-Tamu border posts during 2017–18 comprised mainly agricultural goods, processed foods, and some consumer goods. Indian imports from Myanmar are dominated by betel nuts, beans and legumes, wheat flour, cigarettes, shoes, and clothing items, while exports are mainly lentil seeds, motorcycles and spare parts, bicycles and spare parts, cotton, and traditional Indian dresses.

The prospects for increasing trade through the border post depend on improvements to the AH1 road in Myanmar and upgrading of the facilities and rules for transshipment on both sides of the border. Currently, no trucks are allowed to cross the border, and all cargo is transshipped by manual labor and ferried across in pushcarts.

Zokhawthar-Rih

This is one of the main land border crossing points between India and Myanmar. The Zokhawthar LCS became functional in 2004.[18] The Zokhawthar and Rih posts, which are on opposite sides of the Tiau River, are linked by Bailey Bridge, which was constructed in 2002, prior to the opening of the border crossing point. On the Myanmar side of the LCS, there are two roads connecting Rih-Tiddim (80 km) and Rih-Falam (151 km). Both roads are unpaved and prone to landslides; they require continuous maintenance, especially during the monsoon season. The paving of the Rih-Tiddim Road is likely to be completed in a few years.

Kaladan corridor

An agreement between India and Myanmar was signed in 2008 to develop the Kaladan corridor, which India considers to be of strategic importance to the landlocked states of NER. The government of India is financing the development of the corridor, whose total cost is estimated at $500 million.

The Kaladan corridor, which extends 1,189 km, is a multimodal transport system that connects the Port of Kolkata (India) to Sittwe (Myanmar) by sea, Sittwe to Paletwa (Myanmar) by an inland waterway (Kaladan River), then Paletwa to Zorinpui (Mizoram, India) on the Indo-Myanmar border by road, and from the border to Lawngtlai (India) by a road link. From Lawngtlai, the corridor connects to Aizawl and other centers through the national highway system in India.

The transport infrastructure improvements include building new ports at Sittwe and Paletwa, dredging sections of the Kaladan River, building new roads on both sides of the border, and building new LCSs at the shared border. In addition, other components of the project include the purchase of six IWT barges (each with capacity of 300 tonnes) for transportation of cargo between Sittwe and Paletwa.

Development of the corridor is already quite advanced. The IWT terminal at Paletwa and a port at Sittwe are already substantially completed, while the construction of the roads from Lawngtlai to Zorinpui (90 km) on the India-Myanmar border and from Zorinpui to Paletwa (129 km) in Myanmar is ongoing and expected to be completed by 2020. For transport services, the governments of India and Myanmar signed a framework agreement, the Protocol on Transit Transport, and the Protocol on Maintenance in 2008. Once completed and fully operational, the corridor will reduce the distance between Kolkata and Aizawl by almost 300 km compared with the route through the Siliguri Corridor.

Bangladesh-China-India-Myanmar Economic Corridor

The corridor that connects Myanmar and NER and Bangladesh is a continuation of the main trade corridor linking Myanmar and China. Most of the trade between Myanmar and China is through the Muse border post (Myanmar), where as many as 1,000 trucks cross per day (World Bank 2016). Going westward, the traffic flow between Myanmar and NER is lower, and a significant proportion of it is informal. However, there is already a discernible trend of Chinese manufacturing firms starting to locate inland, with Chinese manufacturers looking at Myanmar and, beyond, at Indian markets. The Bangladesh-China-India-Myanmar Economic Corridor (BCIM-EC) is the only land connectivity corridor that connects India with China through Myanmar and Bangladesh.

The BCIM-EC extends over 2,800 km, encompassing an estimated 440 million people in China's Yunnan province, Bangladesh, Myanmar, NER, and West Bengal in India. It comprises road expressways and high-speed railway connectivity linking Kunming (China), Mandalay (Myanmar), Dhaka (Bangladesh), and Kolkata (India). In NER, the corridor has links to major nodes, including Shillong, Dimapur, Aizawl, Agartala, Nagaon, and Dibrugarh. The BCIM-EC route overlaps with the Trilateral Highway route from Moreh in Manipur to Mandalay in Myanmar.

The corridor has eight pairs of border-crossing stations: four between China and Myanmar, two between Myanmar and India, and two between India and Bangladesh. Operations are currently hampered by several regulatory misalignments, including four international time zones, two different working weeks, four customs systems, two different vehicle driving standards, and four different sets of motor vehicle laws. There are also constraints in transit, as presently only China and India have signed and ratified the Transport Internationaux Routier convention. Bangladesh and Myanmar have yet to sign. Therefore, despite its great potential, the corridor is still to be fully operationalized. Most of the traffic flows on this corridor are currently between pairs of countries, such as Bangladesh-India (NER) and Myanmar-China.

CONCLUSIONS AND POLICY OPTIONS

The connectivity picture of NER reflects the national, historical, and economic contexts of the region. Partly as a result, the region faces long distances and transit times to markets in the rest of India, while connectivity to neighboring countries is inefficient, slow, and generally costly. At the same time, NER states could benefit from leveraging connectivity to exploit the opportunities that Bangladesh and Myanmar in particular offer. After all, NER already has the basic infrastructure, albeit still skeletal, linking it to its neighbors. Although connectivity is largely by road, NER increasingly has extensive networks of rail and air transport that could be interconnected with those of Myanmar and Bangladesh, with significant multiplier effects.

Enhancing connectivity in NER and between NER and neighboring countries will require investments in interoperable infrastructure and services, reforms to regulatory programs, and incentives to the private sector to offer new and higher-quality services. Most of the interventions are at the national level. As such, the national government as well as the NER states should undertake specific reforms. To maximize impact, the private sector, as a direct beneficiary, must be involved. The priority reforms are outlined in the following sections.

Developing logistics hubs and corridors

NER is characterized by thin populations dispersed over difficult terrain. Logistically, that entails thin demand over long distances. To leverage the investments in highways and railways, traffic must be consolidated along a few long-distance corridors and at a few nodes.

As with most economic corridors, formal designation and concerted effort will be needed to increase traffic and encourage a self-reinforcing process of increased capacity and efficiency and volumes of traffic. The costs of improvements and unit costs would then be lower for long-distance shipments. The same principles would apply to air transport, where a hub-and-spokes system can be developed to concentrate volume through a few airports, which would then offer regional and international flights.

Based on the intersections of the traditional and new trade routes, there are three locations that could be developed as logistics hubs for NER:

1. *Guwahati (Assam).* Guwahati has traditionally served as a gateway to NER. It is well connected nationally and within the region. The proposed air connectivity to cities in South Asia and East Asia and beyond will further enhance the centrality of Guwahati as the gateway for NER.
2. *Agartala (Tripura).* The extension of the BG railway network to Agartala and the plans to eventually connect to Chittagong through Sabroom LCS and Akhaura will make the state capital of Tripura another major gateway for NER. Agartala already serves as a major trade node, with use of the road network for bilateral trade with Bangladesh and an entry point for goods moving on the protocol route for inland waterborne trade flows.
3. *Silchar (Assam).* Silchar has emerged as a critical junction, as the Northeast Frontier Railway extends the BG railway network in NER. Silchar is on the Trans-Asian Railway network connecting South Asia and ASEAN,

through Myanmar; it is connected to the protocol waterway route to Bangladesh; and it lies along the Trilateral Highway. As such, the center has the connectivity attributes that can serve as the basis for a logistics cluster for a large part of NER.

To develop these locations into viable and beneficial clusters, it is important to analyze the likely trade flows and functions that each cluster can perform; develop first- and last-mile connectivity links and facilities; engage with the private sector, which will be required to invest in the services and supply chains to be served; make land available at the right locations; and consider other incentives that may be offered to the investors in each potential cluster. Critical services that will be required include those for cold chains, to support the fresh produce that the region produces and of which it could produce more.

Plugging gaps in the transport networks

The government of India is investing heavily in new road, rail, air, water, and border infrastructure. For interoperability of the transport systems, it is important that there be agreement across the various countries on common standards, especially along the major corridors. This will enable vehicles and trains to travel across borders without the need for costly transloading.

Although India and its neighboring countries have a basic interconnected road network, road transport operations are hampered by differences in, for example, market access policies, axle load limits, and quality requirements. Table 3.8 illustrates the differences in axle load limits between India, Bangladesh, Myanmar, and Thailand. The limits in Bangladesh are consistently lower than those in India for the same class of trucks. This could reflect either weaker pavements in Bangladesh or a regulatory legacy under which the limits have not kept pace with recent trends in trucking technology. In any event, the differences in axle load limits are cited as one reason for denying India transit rights across Bangladeshi territory.

Similarly, railways in the region have a combination of meter and BG lines, which impedes cross-border movements. Bangladesh has had to construct both gauges in some parts of the network to interface with the Indian system. Infrastructure differences can be accommodated only through large investments of time and money. However, some of the major constraints lie in the policy choices of the countries. It is important that the countries of the region standardize their infrastructure standards to allow seamless cross-border services.

TABLE 3.8 **Gross vehicle weight limits in Bangladesh and India**
Tonnes

VEHICLE TYPE	BANGLADESH	INDIA[a]	MYANMAR	THAILAND
3 axles (1 front, 2 back)	22.0	21.0	23.0	25.0
4 axles (steering and 3 axles)	25.0	27.0	30.0	30.0
5 axles (3 prime mover, 2 trailer)	38.0	49.0	46.0	45.0
6 axles (3 prime mover, 3 trailer)	41.0	55.0	51.5	50.5
7 axles (3 prime mover, 4 axles)	44.0	n.a.	n.a.	n.a.

Sources: World Bank estimates, data from various sources.
Note: n.a. = not applicable.
a. Revised limits adopted in 2018.

The BBIN Motor Vehicles Agreement (MVA) provides one of the building blocks for uninterrupted traffic flows within the South Asia region and potentially also between South Asia and ASEAN. The ability of vehicles to cross borders is fundamental to greater trade integration. However, in addition to agreements such as the BBIN MVA, it is important for the countries to negotiate complementary reforms in, for instance, road signage, driver training, and insurance.

Improving trade facilitation

The challenges of trade facilitation between NER and neighboring countries are most visible at the land border crossing points. Goods must be transloaded between vehicles of different countries, and the clearance processes are lengthy. As of 2019, for instance, at some border posts with Myanmar, the lack of traffic rights exchange (even on a municipal basis) results in an inefficient transshipment process—goods are carried on carts over distances of more than 500 meters of dirt road. Indian vehicles, however, can go into Nepal and vice versa.[19]

Seamless movement of traffic across borders, which reduces transshipment operations, can bring benefits such as cheaper and more reliable transport and greater cargo security. Some of the common practical issues for land border crossing points are shown in table 3.9.

Along the border with Myanmar, formalizing trade is important. The open practice of smuggling and informal trade (especially of electronic goods coming from China and East Asia) partly explains why the Indian authorities: (1) limit the opening of the border gate to three hours daily; (2) treat the border as an informal facility; and (3) frequently stop access when the level of smuggling becomes too obvious. Eventually, nonstop traffic may bring additional benefits, such as cheaper and more reliable transport and greater cargo security.

TABLE 3.9 Common problems and possible solutions at Land Customs Stations in NER

ISSUE	POSSIBLE INTERVENTION
Access roads to land border crossing points are often narrow with not enough space for vehicles to park on the roadside. This creates congestion and delays, which result in high truck demurrage charges to exporters.	India has built Integrated Check Posts at Agartala and Petrapole and is planning a few others along the border with Bangladesh. However, although the facilities should help address the space constraints, the access road between the two sides is currently not aligned. There should be active engagement between the two sides on development plans.
There is often not enough space or sheds for transloading.	Space for transloading should be larger on the side that is importing more volume. Capacity should be matched to need.
There are differences in border opening hours on the Bangladesh and India sides, and the early closure at 5 p.m. reduces the average workday to 6–7 hours. In addition, there are differences in holidays each week, further reducing the commercial workweek to only two days. Differences in opening hours and holidays are also an issue on borders with other countries.	There is a need to synchronize border opening hours between the two sides. A system of prearrival processing of documents could be introduced to expedite clearance.
There are labor syndicates on both sides of the border that increase transloading costs.	Measures should be taken to abolish syndicate practices at the border posts. Transloading could also be mechanized to improve efficiency.
Customs clears goods only if the complete consignment has arrived.	Processing could be allowed for split consignments.

Source: World Bank.

Myanmar could consider leveraging regional trade at the subnational level. For example, Chin State and Rakhine State have untapped potential for agricultural and fisheries products that could be further developed to meet export demand, particularly from the Bangladeshi and Indian markets. Facilities and access roads at Sittwe Port or Kyaukpyu Port could also be considered for upgrading, to make the ports an additional gateway for Myanmar, particularly for firms in Rakhine State, to access markets in South Asia and Africa. The developments to link these ports through better road infrastructure with the Mandalay-Kalay-Tamu corridor could potentially attract transshipment for trade with China's Yunnan province. Other essential reforms to increase trade between India and Myanmar could include establishing local cross-border traffic rights and identifying options to ease border trade restrictions without compromising security. Training is necessary for border officials and private sector users (customs brokers, transporters, traders, and laborers) on the current trade policy between the two countries and associated processes, as a recent World Bank report highlights (Kathuria 2018).

Modernizing private sector logistics practices

The weaknesses of the logistics practices in NER are reflected in the incidence of postharvest losses. The losses stem from poor handling of products, especially fresh produce, and the long shipment times to markets. Under such circumstances, the quality of packaging and transport is important. In other regions, pallets are widely used in logistics as a convenient way to facilitate the storage, stacking, handling, and transportation of goods. One of the major sources of inefficiency at border posts and ports is the use of manual labor to transload cargo from trucks of one country to those of another. This process could be made more efficient, especially for major shippers, by adopting the use of pallets and deploying mechanized means of transfer, such as forklift trucks. The private sector could be encouraged to invest in handling facilities and warehouses.

In addition to pallets, the penetration of containers into the hinterland of South Asia and especially into NER is limited outside Guwahati. There is currently very little if any containerized movement by road across borders. In Southeast Asia, it takes only a few minutes to transload cargo from the trucks of one country to those of another through the use of containers and the provision of appropriate cranes at the border posts. Some of the cranes are privately owned, and a fee is payable for the transloading operation. Similar approaches could be adopted, especially between Bangladesh and India, where some of the border posts handle significant flows of goods.

Overall, the logistics services markets in NER could also be opened to Bangladeshi operators and vice versa, especially once the railway connectivity to the Port of Chittagong is completed. This will facilitate the smooth clearance and movement of containers at the port to and from destinations across NER.

Introducing a through-transit system

The absence of integrated and modern transit systems has long been an impediment to transit traffic across South Asia. For efficient cross-border movement of cargo, it is essential that roads, rails, and inland waterways operate seamlessly across borders. The shapes of the borders in the region position Bangladesh as a transit country for trade between NER and the rest of India and for Nepal and Bhutan. The movement of vehicles is not possible across borders, whether for transit or goods. Therefore, goods must be offloaded at the border and transferred to vehicles from the other country. This practice is inefficient. The same applies to railways, where locomotives must be changed. The recently adopted BBIN MVA provides a framework (not yet operational) for Indian traffic to cross from the rest of India to the NER states across Bangladesh. Such transit would halve the travel distance, to about 500 km.

A functional through-transit system between the countries of South Asia and between South Asia and ASEAN countries has the potential to transform the trade facilitation environment in the region, especially for the landlocked countries (e.g., ADBI 2015). The problem here is a very specific one that requires a practical transit solution on a few identified road corridors with significant traffic potential. Among the important prerequisites for an operational transit system should be:

- A functional transit procedure through Bangladesh that would allow seamless movement of goods between West Bengal and the NER states of India, with no significant waiting time at the border or en route due to inspections or transloading.
- Adequate mechanisms to enable Bangladesh to recoup the costs associated with the required infrastructure and services, according to universal principles of freedom of transit.

With suitable transit arrangements, some of the road traffic currently moving through the Chicken's Neck in particular could transit across Bangladesh, with significant savings in shipping times.

Tapping the potential of low-cost inland waterways

The challenges to the effective use of the waterways in the region include heavy siltation, shifting channels, lack of adequate depth of water during the lean season, constraints on night navigation, and the absence of other navigation aids in many parts of the channels in the Brahmaputra and Barak Rivers. Links to other forms of connectivity, such as roads and railways, as well as digital connectivity (mobile, phone, and Internet) would also help increase the benefits of the waterways in the region.

Recent developments—such as the signing in 2017 of a memorandum of understanding between Bangladesh and Bhutan on the use of inland waterways for bilateral trade and transit cargo, as well as on passenger and cruise services on the coastal and protocol routes between India and Bangladesh—make it evident that inland navigation is gaining greater traction in the Bay of Bengal subregion. The agreement between India and Bangladesh on the development of a fairway from Sirajganj (Bangladesh) to Daikhowa (India) and between Ashuganj (Bangladesh) and Zakiganj (Bangladesh) on Indo-Bangladesh protocol routes would pave the way for year-round navigation on these routes. This would facilitate bilateral and transit trade, a large part of which will move through NW-2 in India.

Therefore, developing an integrated transport plan with special emphasis on multimodal connectivity would open this isolated region to its neighbors and the rest of the world, with the prospect for substantial gains in economic growth, new livelihood generation, and prosperity, leading to political and social stability. At present, Pandu is the only port with multimodal connectivity in NW-2;

IWAI is presently considering a proposal to develop a multimodal terminal at Joghigopa as well. This will provide Bhutan easier access to NW-2 by road and from there to Bangladesh through waterways. The entry points to India by road could be at Phuentsholing, Gelephu, or Samdrup Jhongkar, and the potential export cargo for Bhutan is boulders, gypsum, and limestone.

Expanding air connectivity

NER is well suited for the production of fresh produce, especially vegetables, fruits, and flowers. It is rich in cultural and natural assets, which makes it an attractive destination for tourists. Its relative strengths in services may enable it to develop into a viable destination for those seeking education and medical services. However, the region is far from the main markets of the rest of India, and connectivity to regional and global markets is limited. As a result, costs are high while shipping times tend to be long and unreliable. Air transport has significant potential to sustain commerce and tourism, and to realize the potential of horticulture and floriculture in the region. Although the approach of developing more airports is quite appropriate, it will need to be accompanied by careful route planning to consolidate shipments and maintain regular schedules to key markets to retain market share. In addition, scheduling is important to ensure the commercial viability of key routes. With respect to network expansion, the proposed direct connectivity with neighbors such as Bangladesh, Myanmar, Nepal, and Thailand should have a significant impact on NER. Exploiting the full potential of regional air connectivity will require supportive policy reforms, especially of visa procedures. This is particularly the case with Bangladesh, which is a main source of medical tourists to India but is not part of the e-visa procedures that India has in place for most other countries.

ANNEX 3A: NER'S TRADE WITH BANGLADESH, 2015–16

		TOP PRODUCTS TRADED	
NO.	NAME OF LCS	EXPORTS	IMPORTS
1	Sutarkandi	Coal and quick lime	Cement, miscellaneous food items, and plastic items
2	Karimganj Steamer & Ferry Station	Ginger, oranges, dry fish, and other citrus fruits	Knitted and crocheted synthetic fabric
3	Mankachar	Coal and boulder stone	Cement, vests, cloaks, and religious books
4	Borsora	Coal and limestone	None recorded
5	Bholaganj	Limestone, boulder stone, and quartz stone	None recorded
6	Dawki	Coal, limestone, raw hides, quartz stone, stone boulders, seasonal fruits, and vegetables	Food items, fire clay, and bricks
7	Shellabazar	Limestone and boulder stone	None recorded
8	Bagmara	Coal	None recorded
9	Dalu	Coal	Cement and synthetic fabrics
10	Ghasuapara	Coal	None recorded
11	Mahendraganj	Coal, crushed stone, boulder stone, dry fish, and ginger	Cotton waste, synthetic fabric, and food products

continued

table continued

		TOP PRODUCTS TRADED	
NO.	NAME OF LCS	EXPORTS	IMPORTS
12	Agartala	Other craft paper, vulcanized rubber tread, and fresh mangoes	Stone, cement, fish, PVC pipe, and furniture
13	Srimantapur	Raw hides, woven fabrics, and synthetic filament	Stone, cement, and plastic polymer sheeting
14	Khowaighat	None recorded	Stone and cement
15	Manu	None recorded	Broken stone, bricks, and cement
16	Muhurighat	None recorded	Stone, bricks, and cement
17	Old Raghnabazar	Citrus fruits	Textile items, cotton vests, and others

Source: World Bank estimates based on data from Indian Customs.
Note: LCS = land customs station; NER = North Eastern Region; PVC = polyvinyl chloride.

NOTES

1. The ranking of major industries in a state has been done according to the value of their gross output. The industry with maximum gross output is ranked first, and others are ranked in descending order of their gross output.
2. The Ministry of Road Transport and Highways of India has taken up the ambitious SARDP-NE for development of the road network in the region. The focus of investment under this program is providing road connectivity to all the district headquarter towns in NER through at least a two-lane highway, as well as providing road connectivity to backward and remote areas, areas of strategic importance, and neighboring countries. SARDP-NE has been planned in two phases, A and B, and covers about 10,141 km. Phase A has been completed, and the work for phase B is ongoing.
3. The destination of this highway on the western side is the state of Gujarat in the western part of India.
4. The cost of transportation by IWT is lower than that for rail and roads. According to calculations based on data from the Ministry of Shipping, the cost of shipping freight is estimated at Rs 1.36 per tonne-kilometer (tkm) for rail, Rs 2.50 per tkm for roads, and Rs 1.06 per tkm for IWT. Ministry of Shipping. 2018. "Operational National Waterways in the Country," online summary (accessed April 12, 2019), http://www.pib.nic.in/Pressreleaseshare.aspx?PRID=1557459.
5. With the growth of the tea industry in the 19th century, these rivers became important carriers of trade. The East India Company started the water route along the Brahmaputra River from Dibrugarh to Kolkata in 1844, and steamships were introduced by the Joint Steamer Company in 1847. At about the same time, Silchar was linked with Kolkata along the Barak-Surma-Meghna navigation channel. However, with the division of the Indian subcontinent in 1947 and then again in 1971, transportation links through Bangladesh were disrupted.
6. Day navigation aids have been installed on the entire 891-km waterway from Dhubri to Sadiya/Oriumghat.
7. Government of India, Ministry of Shipping, Press Release (February 8, 2018), http://pib.nic.in/newsite/PrintRelease.aspx?relid=176384.
8. For details on these initiatives and other developments on enhancing inland and coastal waterway connectivity, see Press Information Bureau, Ministry of Shipping, Government of India, http://pib.nic.in/newsite/PrintRelease.aspx?relid=184384.
9. Instrument Landing System (ILS) technology provides pilots with both vertical and horizontal guidance during an approach to land or aircraft.
10. World Bank calculations based on data from the Direction of Trade Statistics, International Monetary Fund (accessed October 14, 2019), http://data.imf.org/?sk=9D6028D4-F14A-464C-A2F2-59B2CD424B85.
11. World Bank calculations based on data from the Direction of Trade Statistics, International Monetary Fund (accessed October 14, 2019), http://data.imf.org/?sk=9D6028D4-F14A-464C-A2F2-59B2CD424B85.

12. World Bank calculations based on data for 2016, sourced from the World Integrated Trade Solution, on India's major exports to and major imports from ASEAN.

13. See, for example, AIC-RIS (2019) for a detailed study of nontariff measures between ASEAN and India.

14. Tiddim in Myanmar, approximately 75 km from Zokhawthar, is currently functioning as an LCS.

15. Border trade is the "exchange of commodities" by people living along both sides of the international border based on a bilaterally agreed-on list.

16. See Reserve Bank of India, Notification RBI/2015-16/230 (November 5, 2015), http://www .eepcindia.org/download/151106153033.PDF; and Directorate General of Foreign Trade, Public Notice 50/2015-20 (December 17, 2015), http://www.eximguru.com/notifications /rescinding-of-the-public-notice-80646.aspx.

17. Zokhawthar (India)–Rih (Myanmar) is not on the Trilateral Corridor, but the road through this border station connects to the Trilateral Corridor at Kalewa (Myanmar).

18. Champai itself was notified as an LCS in 1994; Zokhawtar was formally notified as an LCS only in 2008.

19. For details, see Consulate General of India, "Vehicle Permit" (accessed April 10, 2019), https://www.cgibirgunj.gov.in/page/detail/179.

REFERENCES

ADB (Asian Development Bank). 2011. "North Eastern State Roads Investment Program." RRP IND 37143-01, ADB, Manila.

ADBI (Asian Development Bank Institute). 2015. "Connecting South Asia and Southeast Asia." ADBI, Manila.

AIC-RIS (ASEAN-India Centre at RIS). 2019. "Non-Tariff Measures: Evidence from ASEAN-India Trade." AIC-RIS, New Delhi.

Brunner, H-P. 2010. *North East India: Local Economic Development and Global Markets.* New Delhi: Sage Publications.

Das, Gurudas, and C. Joshua Thomas, eds. 2016. *Look East to Act East Policy: Implications for India's Northeast.* New Delhi: Routledge.

De, P. 2011. "ASEAN-India Connectivity: An Indian Perspective." In *ASEAN-India Connectivity: The Comprehensive Asia Development Plan Phase II*, edited by Fukunari Kimura and So Umezaki, 96–150. Jakarta: ERIA.

De, P., and Jayanta Kumar Ray. 2013. *India-Myanmar Connectivity: Current Status and Future Prospects.* New Delhi: KW Publishers.

Drewry and Gateway Research. 2018. "Indian Container Market Report 2018" (accessed October 14, 2019). http://containersindia.in/pdf/INDIAN%20CONTAINER%20 MARKET%20REPORT-2018.pdf#page=2.

Government of Bangladesh. 2011. "Economics of Transit Access to India, Nepal and Bhutan through Bangladesh." Unpublished Draft Report of the Sub-Committee 3, Ministry of Commerce, Government of Bangladesh, Dhaka.

Government of India. 2007. "5th Sectoral Summit of the North Eastern Council to Review Air Connectivity Sector Programs in the NER, Issues and Conclusions." Aizawl, Mizoram, May 18–19. Ministry of Development of North Eastern Region, Government of India, New Delhi.

——. 2008. *North Eastern Region Vision 2020.* New Delhi: Ministry of Development of North Eastern Region and North Eastern Council, Government of India (accessed October 14, 2019). http://necouncil.gov.in/sites/default/files/about-us/Vision_2020.pdf.

IWAI and RITES (Inland Waterway Authority of India and Rail India Technical and Economic Services). 2014. *Integrated National Waterways Transportation Grid Study.* Delhi: IWAI.

Kathuria, S., ed. 2018. *A Glass Half Full: The Promise of Regional Trade in South Asia.* Washington, DC: World Bank.

KPMG. 2015. "North East India: Economically and Socially Inclusive Development Strategies." Federation of Indian Chambers of Commerce and Industry, Delhi.

LiveMint. 2019. "As UDAN 3 Takes Off, Guwahati Gets 2 International Flights." January 8. https://www.livemint.com/Politics/T9rD0myShabozUQDGWcOvO/Guwahati-likely-to -be-first-city-to-get-international-flight.html.

MDoNER (Ministry of Development of the North Eastern Region). 2019. "Inland Waterways in NER." MDoNER, Government of India, New Delhi (accessed April 12, 2019). https:// mdoner.gov.in/infrastructure/inland-waterways-in-ner.

Northeast Frontier Railway. 2018. "Northeast Frontier Railway System Map." https://nfr .indianrailways.gov.in/uploads/files/1529387314786-nfr0.pdf.

RIS (Research and Information System for Developing Countries). 2012. "Expansion of North East India's Trade and Investment with Bangladesh and Myanmar: An Assessment of the Opportunities and Constraints." RIS, New Delhi.

Sarma, A., and M. P. Bezbaruah. 2009. "Industry in the Development Perspective of Northeast India." Dialogue, Guwahati, India.

World Bank. 2016. *Myanmar Diagnostic Trade Integration Study: Opening for Business.* Washington, DC: World Bank Group.

4 Quality Standards and Procedures

A PRACTICAL APPROACH FOR EMERGING VALUE CHAINS

MICHAEL FRIIS JENSEN

INTRODUCTION

The North Eastern Region (NER) of India is waking up to a new world of improved connectivity and greater trading opportunities. To exploit trade, producers must upgrade the safety and quality of their products for three reasons. First, domestic middle-income consumers are becoming more aware of product safety issues and demanding better-quality and safer products. Second, growing access to regional markets will grant NER's producers access to global value chains that use more stringent quality standards to coordinate their trade and satisfy distant customers. Third, regulators in India and its neighbors are upgrading food safety and control by tightening both legislation and the currently lax and irregular enforcement.

This chapter explores the extent to which product safety and quality standards and related procedures constrain NER's trade with its neighbors and proposes ways to ease such constraints. Regulatory agencies such as the Food Safety and Standards Authority of India (FSSAI) and the Bangladesh Food Safety Authority (BFSA) have rightly demonstrated a willingness to upgrade food safety regulation. Policy makers, academics, and business communities debate whether nontariff measures (NTMs) rooted in standards, especially those that are not carefully designed, hamper NER's exports or create bigger challenges. This chapter proposes policy reforms and investments that the government and its development partners could consider to ensure that NER benefits from emerging regional trade opportunities. These proposed reforms and investments would also help NER's trade with the rest of India.

The next section presents a model of how standards evolve as a country develops. The model emphasizes that the prevalent production and trading structures determine the available options for upgrading safety and quality standards. The third section describes the production and trading structures in NER. The model focuses on two sets of instruments. The fourth section discusses the first set, which is standards and related procedures, and the fifth section discusses the second set, which addresses value chain interventions. The final section concludes and offers policy recommendations.

MODEL FOR DISCUSSING EVOLVING SAFETY AND QUALITY STANDARDS

The World Bank has produced a model of how food standards evolve with development. The model shows how product standards gradually tighten and give rise to NTMs (figure 4.1). In many developing countries, agricultural markets are traditional wet markets, where consumers judge traded goods using only visual characteristics such as color and size. In these markets, food is procured through long and atomistic value chains dominated by a multitude of producers and market intermediaries. This is the current state of the agricultural market in NER. As income rises and information on quality and safety spreads, quality and safety standards evolve.

First, traders begin to grade products that allow them to target different market niches and demand consistent product quality (figure 4.1, level 2). Later, testing and inspection services emerge to address concerns about pesticide

FIGURE 4.1

Evolution of safety and quality standards

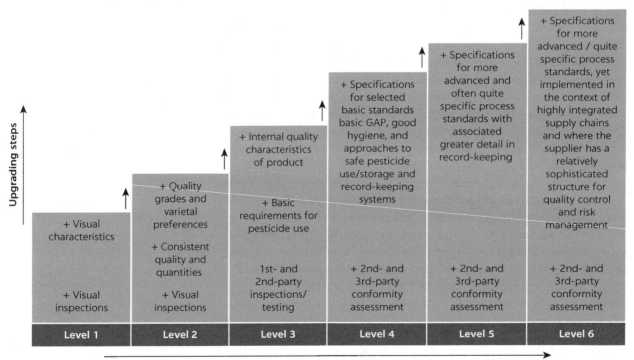

Source: Jaffee, Henson, and Diaz Rios 2011.
Note: GAP = Good Agricultural Practices.

residues in food, for example, which cannot be judged by visual inspection. Over time, the requirements become more stringent, as traders want to manage ever more product characteristics.

In figure 4.1, level 3, buyers introduce criteria for the production process. They demand Good Agricultural Practices (GAP), safe pesticide practices, and record-keeping systems. The buyers set ever more complex quality and safety requirements, ultimately addressing such issues as aflatoxin exposure and environmental management, which require advanced technology and third-party testing and inspection services.

Historically, the transition from level 1 to level 6 has been a decades-long process, although the transition in emerging middle-income countries like China and Brazil has been faster. In developing countries, a dual system may exist for years, with some value chains continuing to supply traditional markets and poor consumers, while other value chains cater to middle-income consumers and export markets.

Upgrading standards should be demand-driven. Demand stems from buyers and the government. Buyers respond to consumers' quest for higher-quality products and quality differentiation by imposing more stringent and exacting quality requirements. Governments respond to calls for safer products from citizens with growing incomes and a rising awareness of food safety issues.

The work to upgrade quality takes place within value chains—for example, farmers learn to apply pesticides correctly, traders store products appropriately, and exporters acquire knowledge of the product standards in foreign markets. Policy makers must always understand the production and trading structures in which these actors work to gauge their potential to upgrade quality. Long and atomistic value chains are more challenging for upgrading quality than short and coordinated ones. To upgrade quality and safety, a country must often change its production and trading structures and introduce instruments such as contract farming, cooperatives, extension services, or other value chain interventions that directly influence quality.

As the demand for quality and safety rises, an economy develops its offering of services such as standards, testing, certification, and inspection—all of which may be produced by private sector firms or government agencies. These services may be produced domestically or imported. In traditional agrarian societies where value chains are long and atomistic, farmers and traders face difficulties in reacting to quality and safety requirements, because they do not have the means to respond or the information does not reach them.

Standards, testing, certification, and inspection establish and reveal such information to producers, consumers, and regulators. Standards describe the quality and safety requirements of a product, while testing, certification, and inspection services are related procedures used to demonstrate that a product conforms to the quality and safety requirements expressed in the standard.

Standards and related procedures in themselves do little to upgrade quality. Consider a village that produces pineapples. Traders pass through the village during the harvest season and buy ripe pineapples. They resell the purchased pineapples to larger traders, which collect sufficient volume to fill large trucks and take the pineapples for sale to consumers in wet markets in a major city located some hundreds of kilometers away from the village. Imagine that a newly established food safety laboratory in the city finds that some of the pineapples have been contaminated with E. coli bacteria. Unfortunately, the trade and production structures are such that it is impossible to trace the contaminated pineapples back to the farms to convey to the farmers that their pineapples are contaminated.

In such a setting, the testing itself does little to upgrade quality. E. coli has likely been transmitted by farmworkers not washing their hands after having been to the toilet. In many villages, poor hygiene is common, and the hurdle for quality upgrading is how to improve hygiene. In this example, the use of testing alone, without a value chain intervention such as a hand-washing campaign, cannot upgrade quality.

PRODUCTION AND TRADING STRUCTURES IN NER

The literature tells us little about how NER's economic structures affect the ability to comply with standards. Fafchamps, Hill, and Minten (2007, 2008), however, study how traditional structures elsewhere in India interact with quality control. They look at nonstaple foods—such as mangoes, tomatoes, and turmeric—and conduct surveys in Tamil Nadu, Uttar Pradesh, Maharashtra, and Odisha to establish the most important quality requirements and how farmers and traders comply.

The authors find that Indian value chains inadequately transmit information on crop characteristics. Growers receive a price premium when they dry, grade, and pack their produce, but the study finds that value chains do not transmit information about crop salubrity or agricultural practices and that growers are not encouraged to follow agricultural practices that upgrade quality. The long and atomistic value chains that dominate Indian agriculture prevent the transmission of information. The authors find very little evidence of horizontal or vertical integration and little use of the modern forms of organization that are needed to upgrade quality.

As in the states studied by Fafchamps, Hill, and Minten (2007, 2008), the agriculture sector in NER is traditional. Small farmers produce bulk products that are traded through myriad small traders. Most of the production caters to local markets, while a few commodities, like Assamese tea, are exported. Some products target niche markets for the "discerning" Indian consumer who is quality conscious.

Traditional farming and local consumer preference for cheap products influence quality. Studies of pork and dairy products in Nagaland and Assam demonstrate quality problems. Only 6 percent of the pork sampled in Nagaland complied with government standards (Fahrion et al. 2014). Assamese dairy consumers rely on informal markets dominated by traditional milk market agents. Processing units are small and operate at low capacity. Agents lack training, and their operations suffer from poor hygiene and milk adulteration. Such problems could be addressed by training in hygiene, milk quality, and business practices (ILRI 2007; Lapar et al. 2014). ILRI (2007) observes that consumer awareness of milk quality and safety is rising, and quality assurance measures such as branding, regulation, and monitoring should link traditional agents to formal outlets. The poor quality of locally processed milk is a key barrier for the Assamese dairy industry.

Nonetheless, younger agro-entrepreneurs are developing high-quality products for niche markets and are connecting NER farmers with discerning consumers across India. In addition, selected major Indian companies are investing in NER agribusinesses, as exemplified by the Tata Group, which has invested in a modern spice-processing facility in Assam.

Niche markets for discerning consumers are developing around such products as organics, "elephant-friendly" tea, Lakadong turmeric with high curcumin content, ginger with high oleoresin content, large cardamom, Bhut Jolokia and Naga Chilies, varieties of Joha rice and black rice, rice produced under a geographical indication, high-quality pork products, and ecofriendly bamboo products such as bamboo wood.

Organic production is receiving attention from producers, buyers, and the government. NER farmers use fewer chemical pesticides and synthetic fertilizers, making their produce "de facto organic." To commercialize this advantage, farmers need certification. India has a government plan for organic certification titled the National Program for Organic Production (NPOP). Traders doubt whether export markets recognize the Indian program. Firms search for high-value markets to offset NER's disadvantages such as high transport costs. Most products for quality-conscious consumers are produced and traded in small volumes, often by struggling firms, and may require testing and certification to distinguish them from bulk products.

STANDARDS AND RELATED PROCEDURES

Standards

As the Indian central authority on food safety, FSSAI is working to upgrade Indian food safety standards and introduce international best practices in domestic and trade controls. This drive toward more stringent food control is a necessity. In 2015, the World Health Organization (WHO) published the first *Estimates of the Global Burden of Foodborne Diseases* (WHO 2015). At the global level, WHO estimated that 600 million—almost one in 10 people—fall ill after eating contaminated food and 420,000 die every year. Diarrheal diseases are the most common, causing 550 million people to fall ill and 230,000 deaths every year. Children under five years bear 40 percent of the foodborne disease burden, with 125,000 deaths every year. Developing countries bear the brunt of foodborne diseases. Africa and Southeast Asia, which is defined by WHO to include India, have the highest incidence of illness and associated death rates.

Regional trading partners are also upgrading food control. Bangladesh enacted a new food law in 2013 and created a new agency, BFSA, two years later. This agency is charged with introducing strengthened and modernized food safety regulations. The Food and Drug Administration in Myanmar is introducing risk-based import control as part of a drive toward strengthening food safety. At the regional level, the South Asian Association for Regional Cooperation is working toward harmonizing food standards across South Asia, an initiative supported by India in the newly adopted Indian National Strategy for Standardization.

Today, the ability to manage food safety is primarily a commercial imperative in value chains catering to high-end domestic markets in India and selected export markets. In the future, depending on the speed with which regulations are upgraded and consumers push for increased food safety, many more value chains will be influenced by this trend.

In some cases, producers could benefit from standards that convey the quality characteristics of their products. Bamboo from NER could benefit from investment in the development of standards. Bamboo is used relatively less often than other building materials due to a lack of reliable knowledge of its characteristics (Trujillo and Jangra 2016). Bamboo is difficult to use in construction, because structural design codes and standards are based on the mechanical properties of materials like timber. Grading standards classify materials according to their properties and thus inform potential users about the quality characteristics of the material, which allows them to identify what they need. The grading of bamboo is not done systematically, in NER or elsewhere, and that may explain why bamboo is today a marginal product in construction. Engineers are unsure of the precise properties of the bamboo they might source and thus avoid using it in favor of better-understood materials.

In 2018, the International Network for Bamboo and Rattan, in collaboration with the International Standards Organization, published bamboo-grading standards,[1] with funding from China. The new standard—ISO 19624/2018—will assist in spreading knowledge about the benefits of bamboo in construction and how to use it.

A country may assist commercial product development by developing standards. Government food control may strengthen the value chain by providing incentives to manage food safety. Grace (2015) observes that in China and Vietnam, changing industry structures, rapid market development, rapidly changing prices of products and inputs, low profit margins, lack of bargaining power of key players, and lack of government support to stabilize markets all put high pressure on value chain actors to cut corners and sacrifice food safety. In a developing value chain in this situation, the absence of food control allows high prices to bring in a rush of investment that increases production, which lowers prices and dampens investment until supply is reduced again, which allows prices to spike once more, and the cycle goes on. This volatility reduces the incentive to invest in food safety and threatens access to markets where food safety management is crucial. Food control by the government can help strengthen value chains by providing more stable incentives to manage food safety.

For most exports, Indian standards play a minor role. International buyers and importing countries' regulations define the standards and regulations with which Indian exporters must comply. Spices are an exception. The Spices Board of India has created mandatory testing requirements that guarantee that Indian spices comply with importing countries' regulations (Spices Board of India, undated). This policy safeguards the global reputation of Indian spices. The requirements regulate aflatoxin levels, chemicals such as the prohibited dyestuff Sudan, and microbiological parameters—issues that have caused high-income markets to reject Indian spices in the past. Despite such exceptions, the most important requirements for NER exporters remain a combination of buyer standards and importing-market technical regulations. The Spices Board of India enforces export control to assure international buyers that the safety and quality of Indian spices meet their standards.

Private food standards increasingly influence competitiveness and market access (Clarke 2010). Indian actors have developed private standards such as Trustea, which was developed by multiple private stakeholders under the leadership of the government's Tea Board of India. This standard addresses food safety parameters such as pesticide use and other parameters linked to the social and environmental effects of growing tea. In the future, such private initiatives are likely to proliferate. They serve dual purposes. First, they market quality and safety by identifying parameters such as taste and pesticide use; then, through traceability and certification, they preserve and transmit the information embodied in these parameters throughout the value chain. Second, they support the government's regulatory mandate by enforcing food safety and similar social concerns, often in ways that are complementary to the efforts already being undertaken by regulatory agencies like FSSAI. It is likely that such agencies will include private initiatives directly in future regulation. For example, agencies may choose to accept aspects of private certification—when done by independent third-party bodies—as proof of compliance with regulations. The future success of private initiatives like Trustea will depend on the credibility of the standard-creation and certification processes.

The private codes developed to source bamboo by large buyers like IKEA are another example of private standards. Managers of a bamboo-processing facility visited in June 2018 indicated that they had discussed supplying a large international buyer but faced financial difficulties. They estimated that the facility would have to incur certification costs and make changes to its processing unit at a total cost of $220,000 before it would be competitive as a supplier to large international buyers. As discussed in the analysis of bamboo conducted as part of this study (Manghnani 2019), IKEA, for example, has its own standard, called the IWAY Forestry Standard, which includes bamboo. The Forest Stewardship Council, another private initiative, also covers bamboo. The Indian government could support NER firms' access to markets where such private standards dominate in two ways. First, for International Standards Organization standards, the government could influence the standard-setting process by supplying information and other inputs that would ensure that the resulting standards properly include NER advantages. Second, the government could support the implementation of private standards that would link NER producers with global value chains by providing financial and technical support.

Testing and certification

India's overall capacity to provide testing services—by the government or private suppliers—has been increasing rapidly with the growth and diversification of the Indian economy. Private firms, including multinationals like SGS and Bureau Veritas, offer a variety of testing services in the main growth centers in India.

Food imports to India are subject to the requirements of both FSSAI and the Bureau of Indian Standards (BIS). FSSAI regulates the import of food and domestic food safety. BIS has put some processed food under its mandatory certification program. The Food Safety and Standards Act of 2006 consolidated the responsibility for food safety within FSSAI, yet overlaps with other bodies such as BIS still exist. The requirements for powdered and condensed milk illustrate the overlaps. For such products, producers must meet FSSAI regulations and the mandatory standards of BIS. Both sets of rules include requirements for hygiene, additives, and limits on contaminants (Yang 2017).

For imported food, FSSAI relies on testing at FSSAI-notified laboratories. Imported food can be tested to meet FSSAI requirements at the border or in the exporting country. If tested at the border, an officer (commonly a customs officer acting on behalf of FSSAI) takes a sample and sends it to the nearest FSSAI-notified laboratory (which may be far away) and awaits the test results before releasing the food products. Only FSSAI-notified laboratories may test abroad. In that case, the manufacturer sends a sample to the notified laboratory in its country and submits the testing results at the border; customs checks only the documentation.

BIS controls some imported manufactured products. Such imports fall under the BIS mandatory certification program. A foreign manufacturer applies to BIS for a license and sends samples to a BIS-recognized laboratory. BIS inspects the manufacturer, and if the inspection and testing of samples are satisfactory, BIS grants the foreign manufacturer a license giving it the right to use the Indian Standard mark. The manufacturer's exports to India are then accompanied by the appropriate documentation, and the import procedures consist of checking for this documentation and the correct quality mark on the product.

The situation today in NER

NER is poorly equipped with services to ensure compliance. The region has few laboratories, and access to certification and inspection services is poor. Government and private suppliers of services are fewer than in the rest of India.

A range of government bodies provide limited services in NER. The National Accreditation Board for Testing and Calibration Laboratories (NABL) provides accreditation to laboratories on assessment of their competence according to established criteria, including international standards and guidelines.[2] NABL has accredited 39 laboratories in Assam, and one each in the states of Manipur, Tripura, Meghalaya, and Sikkim (NABL 2018). The scope of many of the laboratories, including the ones in Assam, is narrow and not relevant for exporters. The accreditation for the single laboratory in Manipur, for example, is for unspecified chemical analysis of water only.

FSSAI has not notified any laboratories in NER for testing against its food safety regulations. According to FSSAI's website, the nearest notified laboratories are five laboratories in Kolkata. FSSAI has acknowledged the unsatisfactory status of Indian food safety laboratories and has initiated a $75 million India-wide upgrading and investment program for food laboratories, including in all eight states of NER.

The Spices Board of India provides services similar to testing. It is an agency under the Ministry of Commerce and Industry for the development and world-wide promotion of Indian spices. It runs seven quality evaluation laboratories, all located near the major Indian spice production areas and all outside NER.

Similarly, the Export Inspection Council (EIC), another government agency responsible for export quality control, has no facilities in NER. EIC notifies commodities subject to quality control and inspection prior to export, establishes standards of quality, and specifies how to control quality.[3] EIC operates five Export Inspection Agencies in Chennai, Delhi, Kochi, Kolkata, and Mumbai and 30 suboffices. These agencies and offices are in important ports and industrial centers in India. EIC has established its own network of laboratories and has approved external laboratories for the certification of some exports, such as certain spices. These laboratories may be government-operated or private. The nearest EIC facilities to NER are in Kolkata.

The private sector is as important a supplier of testing services as the government. Private firms, including multinationals like SGS and Bureau Veritas, offer services in NER only through their laboratories located outside the region, typically in Kolkata. For example, SGS has an officer stationed at the export zone in Guwahati, who samples produce (mainly tea) and sends the samples to the firm's laboratory in Kolkata. Kolkata is the nearest hub for such commercial services. Buyers of spices, such as exporters, often carry out testing as well. Spices are not exported directly from NER, but through exporters situated elsewhere in India, such as Mumbai. Exporters source NER spices through local traders and test them in Mumbai.

Certification bodies are also rare in NER. Organic certification is needed to commercialize the "de facto organic" nature of spices and other horticultural products from NER. Two systems of organic certification exist. One is Indian organic certification under the NPOP, which, according to interviews with firms, is recognized in the local Indian markets and valued by the Indian consumer but not by export markets. The other comprises trusted international systems that provide access to markets in the European Union and the United States. One strongly export-oriented farmer who was interviewed would not opt for the Indian system, but worked to be certified to the Swiss Bio Suisse organic standard by the multinational quality assurance firm's office in Kolkata.

Institutional structures in Assam

The State Public Health Laboratory (SPHL) in Guwahati (Assam) is the primary laboratory that the government of Assam uses for regulatory purposes. The governments of Arunachal Pradesh, Meghalaya, Mizoram, and Sikkim and FSSAI also use it. The SPHL can test only for simple physical parameters. FSSAI plans to upgrade the SPHL by installing additional equipment, including equipment for pesticide residue analysis, as part of its India-wide laboratory upgrade program. Private firms procure testing services from other, mainly private, laboratories. During fieldwork in Assam in June 2018, investigators found that most of the private firms that were interviewed were not aware of the SPHL. The SPHL is supplemented by a mobile laboratory provided by FSSAI under its Food Safety on Wheels program. This mobile laboratory conducts simple tests for common adulterants in milk, water, edible oil, and similar commonly used food items. State functionaries use the mobile laboratory to conduct outreach and surveillance activities in remote areas and to increase public awareness of food safety, hygiene, and healthy eating habits.[4]

The Indian Institute of Food Processing Technology in Guwahati also plans to offer food testing in the near future. The institute is building a food laboratory that will be able to test for most food safety parameters, including pesticide residues and heavy metals. Testing for mycotoxins will come at a later stage. The parent ministry, the Ministry of Food Processing Industries, has granted Rs 3.5 million ($0.05 million) for the food laboratory.

Furthermore, the Assam Industrial Development Corporation plans to establish a regional food-testing laboratory as part of the North East Mega Food Park in Nalbari. The corporation will invest Rs 86 million ($1.25 million) in the laboratory.[5] The food park is still being developed, although a handful of firms have started operations; the food laboratory is still under construction.

The Department of Food Engineering and Technology at Tezpur University in Tezpur (Assam) has a food quality control laboratory used mainly for research. The National Research Centre on Pig, under the Indian Council of Agricultural Research in Guwahati, also has a laboratory that primarily targets meat testing.

Institutional structures in Tripura

Fieldwork undertaken in June 2017 in Tripura illustrates the demand for testing that arises from trade between NER and Bangladesh. The Agartala (Tripura)–Akhaura (Bangladesh) Integrated Check Post is a significant gateway for trade between the two countries. The demand for testing is mainly for imports into NER. FSSAI regulation requires that food imports be tested, and larger private importers' own quality systems sometimes require that food be tested. The low level of exports from Tripura make it difficult to assess the demand for testing for exports.

In Tripura, four laboratories were active or under construction in June 2018. The Tripura Industrial Development Corporation Ltd. has established a food-testing laboratory in the Food Park at Bodhjungnagar Industrial Complex in Agartala—the first NABL-accredited food testing laboratory in NER. The laboratory has not been notified by FSSAI and has very limited capacity. NABL has accredited it only for simple chemical tests of certain cereals, sugar, and iodized salt. The laboratory does not test essential food safety parameters, and it does not undertake microbiological testing. It has acquired equipment for gas chromatography for pesticide residue testing but lacks the supplies of chemical inputs to use the equipment. The food safety laboratory has a staff of three and tests only 15 to 20 samples per month.

The Regional Food Laboratory in Agartala, under the Health and Family Welfare Department of the Government of Tripura, is another food laboratory in Tripura. Recently, the Health and Family Welfare Department has issued tenders for equipment for the laboratory. The nature of the equipment suggests that the laboratory will soon be able to undertake several chemical and microbiological tests, including testing for pesticide residues and heavy metals. NABL has not accredited it. FSSAI has registered the Regional Food Laboratory as the state laboratory for Tripura but has not notified it.

Other laboratories include the State Level Water Testing Laboratory and a laboratory under construction at the Mega Food Park near Agartala. NABL has accredited the State Level Water Testing Laboratory to test surface water, groundwater, and drinking water. The Mega Food Park laboratory will test food, but the scope of these future testing facilities is unknown.

The private sector does not use government services. A food processor interviewed in Agartala used its own laboratory to test for quality management. That a major food processor avoids using government services shows the private sector's low trust in the quality of such services.

Lessons from the Bangladeshi export market

In Bangladesh, many food regulations are enforced only partially (if at all) at the border. The Bangladesh Standards and Testing Institution (BSTI) is mandated to control food imports, but only for a subset of imported processed food products. BSTI exercises its mandate through mandatory standards. Table 4.1 lists the food products that have been brought under mandatory certification.

BSTI's control is most likely weakly implemented. BSTI employs a total of only 65 inspectors to ensure compliance with all mandatory standards (covering industrial goods and processed foods), domestically and at the border. BSTI reports that all consignments are inspected using risk profiling to lessen the enforcement burden. Clearly, 65 inspectors is a small number for a country with 160 million inhabitants (Jensen 2016). Generally, food safety authorities face severe financial and staff shortages, making it impossible for them to enforce all the rules. BSTI plans to create a network of border laboratories to strengthen the enforcement of its mandate on the control of imports.

BSTI's mandatory standards likely regulate parameters, such as color or size, that are not recognized by the World Trade Organization's (WTO's) Agreement on Application of Sanitary and Phytosanitary Measures. Previous work on yogurt standards, for example, revealed that the BSTI standard for yogurt did not address food safety concerns (Jensen 2016). BFSA will be reviewing all Bangladeshi food standards, comparing them with the Codex Alimentarius and similar international standards (BFSA 2019).

TABLE 4.1 **Food products for which BSTI has set mandatory standards**

Mustard oil	Edible palm oil	Fortified edible palm olein
Refined sugar	Toffees	Sweetened and unsweetened condensed filled milk
Suji (semolina)	Chilies, whole and ground	
Wheat atta	Ice cream	Cumin powder
Maida	Coriander powder	Fortified edible rice bran oil
Bread	Noodles	Dextrose monohydrate
Biscuits	Carbonated beverages	Liquid glucose (glucose syrup)
Lozenges	Curry powder	Honey
Canned and bottled fruits	Iodized salt	Edible sunflower oil
Fruit squashes	Drinking water	Canned pineapple
Fruit cordial	Natural mineral water	Infant formula and formulas for special medical purposes intended for infants
Sauce (fruit or vegetable)	Lassi (yoghurt drink)	
Fruit and vegetable juices	Instant noodles	Processed cereal-based food for infants and young children
Tomato paste	Chips and crackers	Milk powder and cream powder
Fermented vinegar	Chanachur	Sugar
Concentrated fruit juice	Refined palm olein	Fermented milk
Fruit syrup	Cakes	Pickled fruits and vegetables
Tomato ketchup	Soft drink powder	Jams, jellies, and marmalades
Banaspati	Lachsa semai	Butter
Butter oil and ghee	Pasteurized milk	Sweetened condensed milk
Soyabean oil	Fortified soybean oil	Black tea
Turmeric powder	Fortified edible palm oil	Instant tea in solid form
Wheat bran	Fortified edible sunflower oil	

Source: BSTI Standards Catalogue 2018.

The Bangladeshi food safety system is very complex. The chair of BFSA reported that at least 18 ministries are involved in food safety (New Age 2017). The Customs Authority tests for formalin in selected fresh food products, including fresh fruit, milk, and aquaculture products. Customs sends samples to the Bangladesh Council of Scientific and Industrial Research laboratories. This process may take three working days (USDA 2016). BFSA plans to tighten Bangladeshi food safety regulation, which until now has been undertaken by such other authorities as BSTI and the Dhaka City Corporation.

For about a decade, Bangladesh has raised the issue that India stops processed food imports at land border posts and imposes testing requirements. The process of sending samples to laboratories, typically in Kolkata, analyzing them, and finally releasing the consignment takes several weeks and sometimes months. In April 2017, FSSAI issued a notification recognizing testing and certification by BSTI for imports of 21 Bangladeshi food products into India.[6] The notification means that imports of the 21 products already tested in Bangladesh will be subject only to risk-based sampling for testing by India.

Unfortunately, as of July 2018, this agreement had not facilitated imports into India. An exporter reported that BSTI did not have the capacity to test the volumes of processed food exported to India. BSTI is reported to take 21 days to issue a microbiological report after the submission of samples. BSTI fees are about twice as high as the testing fees on the Indian side. The low capacity, waiting times, and high fees may prompt exporters to let their products be tested on the Indian side of the border.

Are NTMs associated with standards, and are related procedures burdensome?

In a study of India-Bangladesh trade, CUTS (2019) analyzes the food safety standards in the two countries. For example, both countries set standards for fruit juices. They both regulate two classes of contaminants: heavy metals and other contaminants. In heavy metals, India regulates lead, tin, zinc, cadmium, mercury, and methyl mercury, while Bangladesh regulates only the first three of these. Of these three, it is only for zinc that India and Bangladesh apply the same maximum admissible level (5 parts per billion). India regulates a series of other contaminants: agaric acid, hydrocyanic acid, hypericin, safrole, and aflatoxins. Bangladesh also regulates these substances, except aflatoxins, and in addition regulates acrylonitrile and vinyl chloride monomer. Both countries set the same maximum admissible levels for the four contaminants they both regulate.

CUTS (2019) observes that only rarely are standards identical in the two countries. Given that India and Bangladesh develop food standards using separate processes, without consultation, and with many parameters that may influence food safety, it is no surprise that the standards often diverge. Neither country strictly refers to the Codex Alimentarius or other international standards that could provide a uniform reference point.

Any divergence—even in a single parameter—in food standards between two countries may establish nontariff barriers. On this aspect, the literature agrees. The degree to which diverging standards result in trade frictions is uncertain, however. Media stories and contributions to the literature frequently promote the belief that standards and their related regulations cause significant trade frictions (for example, Basher 2013; CUTS 2013, 2014, 2019; De and Majumdar 2014; Dhar et al. 2011; Islam 2011; Rahman et al. 2012).

Food safety regulation is not strictly enforced at the India-Bangladesh border (or domestically), and much trade remains informal. For instance, although BSTI in Bangladesh has several mandatory standards for food items that may be relevant for exporters in NER—such as spices, dairy, and processed horticultural products (table 4.1)—the degree to which these mandatory standards are implemented and become burdensome for traders is uncertain. It is likely that the standards are not strictly implemented due to BSTI's capacity problems.

Taneja (2018) suggests that standards and related issues do not pose a big challenge for trade between India and its neighbors. The study examines NTMs in bilateral trade between Bangladesh and India and between India and Nepal in selected products: exports of tea, cardamom, and medicinal and aromatic plants from Nepal to India; exports of processed foods, ready-made garments, and jute bags from Bangladesh to India; exports of pharmaceutical raw materials from India to Bangladesh; and exports of pharmaceuticals from India to Nepal. The study identifies procedural obstacles perceived by exporters in meeting requirements related to sanitary and phytosanitary standards (SPS) and technical barriers to trade (TBT), as captured through a survey. Taneja (2018) measures the restrictiveness of an NTM by the score provided by respondents on a scale of 1 to 5, where 1 indicates that the measure is least restrictive ("very easy" to comply with) and 5 that it is most restrictive ("very hard" to comply with).[7] The questionnaire seeks restrictiveness scores on technical requirements and conformity assessment. Taneja (2018) finds that Indian exports show an overall NTM restrictiveness score for a particular product in the range of 1.3 to 1.8 (somewhere between "easy" and "very easy"). The highest restrictiveness score, 1.84, is found for processed food exported from Bangladesh to India. Here, the study finds that "testing requirements" under conformity assessment measures score 2.5 (between "easy" and "average").

What will the future bring?

Diverging standards will likely result in nontariff barriers to trade in the future. India and Bangladesh are moving toward improving food safety regulations and tightening enforcement. Without policy coordination and greater application of trade facilitation instruments like harmonization, mutual recognition, and equivalence, increasingly stringent and diverging standards will most likely become a source of trade friction in the future. For example, BFSA has begun a program of harmonizing Bangladeshi food safety standards with those of the Codex Alimentarius by inviting national experts to participate in a review of Bangladesh's food standards.

Several government bodies plan to expand food testing services in NER, including in Assam and Tripura. But they are not coordinating their investment plans, which risks wasting resources through duplication. Duplication also jeopardizes the future sustainability of the individual laboratories, because there may not be enough work for all the new or upgraded laboratories to operate at an efficient scale. Fewer laboratories operating at higher capacity would generate a higher return on investment and ensure that the food analysts' skills stay sharp as they conduct the same tests with greater frequency.

How FSSAI's policies on food control, including import control, evolve will influence the configuration of investments in testing capacity. FSSAI has expressed a willingness to move to a greater use of testing in the exporting country by negotiating mutual recognition agreements. This policy, when implemented, will decrease the demand for testing at the border.

When questioned during fieldwork in June 2017, FSSAI stated that it would use risk profiling for food imports and move away from the current approach of attempting 100 percent inspection and testing. In April 2017, FSSAI had issued a notification recognizing testing and certification by BSTI for imports of 21 Bangladeshi food products into India. FSSAI stated that this would be followed by a general policy to create mutual recognition and equivalence agreements, as recommended by the two WTO agreements that regulate how countries may apply technical regulations and standards on trade: the Agreement on the Application of Sanitary and Phytosanitary Measures (SPS Agreement) and the Agreement on Technical Barriers to Trade (TBT Agreement). Food safety measures are regulated by the SPS Agreement, while food standards that do not regulate food safety are regulated by the TBT Agreement. These agreements strongly encourage the use of trade facilitation instruments such as mutual recognition and equivalence. FSSAI would recognize the equivalence of testing laboratories in neighboring countries if such laboratories were accredited by an internationally recognized accreditation body and met additional FSSAI requirements. Such testing laboratories could be government or private (Bhaskar 2017).[8]

Some testing on imports will still be necessary—in exceptional cases, FSSAI might expect fraud or not trust the authorities in the

Example of an import program involving additional testing: EU border control for okra and curry leaves from India

The European Union imports most plant products, subject only to documentary control. However, some risky plant products are regulated more stringently.

The European Union's alert system has observed excessive pesticide residues in imports of okra and curry leaves from India. Thus, okra and curry leaves are subject to a special regulation (European Commission 2009):

- Indian okra and curry leaves can be imported only at specifically designated points of entry that are equipped to undertake the necessary controls.
- Importers must notify the entry point of the arrival of a consignment at least one day in advance.

- The consignments must be accompanied by analytical results of testing done in the producing countries (for example, by the Spices Board of India for curry leaves) and a health certificate.
- The European Union authority checks the documentation at the entry point.
- Twenty percent of the consignment is drawn randomly and becomes subject to pesticide residue analysis.
- The consignment is released for sale within the European Union after the authority is satisfied with the documents and any testing.
- The costs of the controls are borne by the importer.

Sources: European Commission 2009, 2014.

exporting countries. Box 4.1 illustrates an example of a risk-based program applied by the European Union for imports of okra and curry leaves from India.

How the testing procedures can be optimally organized—whether, for example, the testing should take place at the border or inland and whether the testing laboratories should be government or private or both—needs to be carefully analyzed.

Some argue that trade would be facilitated by investing in laboratories at the border. Dhar et al. (2011), for example, argue that testing at the border itself would speed up the process of releasing goods that otherwise would have to wait longer for the results of testing done elsewhere.

International best practice advises caution when investing in laboratories. In a guide on risk-based import control, the Food and Agriculture Organization of the United Nations (FAO) observes that delivering laboratory services is very costly for a government, a fact that should push the government to assess all options for accessing laboratory services (FAO 2016). FAO advises that the government may establish government laboratories, use third parties, or both. FAO discourages authorities from establishing dedicated import food control laboratories. Instead, government agencies should share laboratory services. This implies that investing in laboratories at the border is likely to be a suboptimal strategy: not only are they likely to be used less intensively than if they were located nearer to the production centers, they would also increase border congestion.

VALUE CHAIN INTERVENTIONS

Upgrading the quality of exports from NER is likely to require value chain interventions that target improvement in the quality of products and increased production of such quality products, along with investments to develop testing and certification services, while also working to reduce the burden of restrictive NTMs.

The prevalent traditional production and trading patterns in NER suggest that there is a need to focus more on value chain interventions to improve quality than on investments to upgrade standards and their related procedures to provide quality assurance for existing products. This is illustrated in this section through the examples of spices and pineapples.

Spices

A series of parameters—such as taste, color, pesticide residue content, traces of adulteration with Sudan dyes, and microbiological characteristics—influence the quality of spices. NER chilies, for example, are known to have a high capsaicin content (the component that makes chilies hot). The Bhut Jolokia, or "ghost chili," originating in NER, has been recognized as one of the world's strongest chilies, and this variety has become valuable in international markets for its capsaicin content. The values of these quality parameters are determined by cultivation and trading practices. Testing and certification will reveal the value of the quality parameters but will do little to change those values. If the spices produced are contaminated with dirt or other material, are not the varieties in demand in regional and long-distance international markets, or are not dried properly, causing mold to grow and produce aflatoxins, laboratory testing will reveal only that there is a quality problem; it will not solve the problem.

The Spices Board of India offers development programs that improve the quality of spices by addressing cultivation, harvest, and post-harvest practices. The Spices Board reports that unhygienic practices sometimes lead to poor quality from microbiological contamination or the presence of dirt. The Spices Board supplies plastic sheets at a subsidy to small growers to allow drying of spices off the ground. In a similar attempt to improve pepper quality, the Spices Board promotes the use of mechanical threshers that will end the traditional practice of separating pepper berries from the spikes by trampling under the feet, which may introduce microbiological contaminants and dirt. The threshers are also subsidized. The Spices Board runs several such development activities aimed at improving the quality of Indian spices throughout the country.[9]

Testing may be used to identify problems in the supply chain and provide incentives to solve them. Adulteration with Sudan dyes is a frequently encountered problem that causes high-income countries to reject import shipments. Therefore, testing for the presence of such adulteration is mandatory in India. Testing identifies the problem, but other interventions are needed to solve it. Extension services in the form of advice on the prevailing standards in foreign markets and alternative ways to raise the value of spices instead of using banned coloring agents can help address the problem.

Pineapples

Pineapples provide another illustration of a typical quality problem in NER. Assam is the second-largest producer of pineapples in India, next to West Bengal. Tripura is another state in NER for which pineapples have been historically important. The market for pineapples is primarily local and to some extent regional, including some pockets of India outside NER.

Chinzakhum (2014) analyzes the production and marketing of pineapples in Cachar, one of the major pineapple-producing districts in Assam. The markets are unregulated and unorganized, and myriad small farmers sell their pineapples to intermediaries such as commission agents, wholesalers, and retailers.

Chinzakhum (2014) identifies many marketing problems. Some of these are related to quality, although none to a lack of testing and certification facilities. First, infrastructure is deficient, with most pineapple growers connected to markets only by bridle paths or kutcha roads. Second, losses are caused by poor post-harvest treatment, notably the lack of cooling technology, such as refrigerated vans for transport, appropriate packing houses, and cold storage facilities. The lack of cold storage and transportation leads to spoiling of the highly perishable fruit. High perishability coupled with poor post-harvest treatment reduces quality and shelf life and severely limits the distance that the produce may travel to end consumers.[10] Other problems identified by Chinzakhum (2014) include taxation and other costs imposed by local authorities and wide price fluctuations; the latter are typically caused by the seasonal nature of the crop, high perishability, and isolated markets.

The dominance of smallholders makes quality upgrading challenging. In Cachar district, smallholders dominate pineapple cultivation. The average area devoted to pineapples by the surveyed farmers was 1.5 hectares. Direct marketing to distant end markets by individual farmers is infeasible because of the small scale of production. Chinzakhum (2014) also finds that there is a lack of unity and organizational talent among growers, preventing the formation of a cluster that could promote collective action. The prevalent agrarian structure sets a strong role for market intermediaries, and farmers complain about their lack of buying power against the intermediaries. Value chain innovations such as contract farming and more direct vertical links capable of providing extension services, finance, and quality management are made difficult by the agrarian structure.

CONCLUSIONS AND POLICY OPTIONS

In NER, production and trading structures are primarily traditional, dominated by small units and atomistic value chains exercising little vertical coordination. These structures are not conducive to upgrading quality. In such an environment, quality upgrading is a process of building value chain capacity to supply the safety and quality parameters demanded by consumers and buyers and mandated by government, and to develop the capacity of quality infrastructure to demonstrate compliance.

The demand for safer and higher-quality products is currently limited by low incomes and poor connectivity to international markets. Niche products for discerning consumers are developing, although their volumes remain very small.

The region is waking up to a new world of improved connectivity as well as greater trading opportunities. These opportunities will be accompanied by pressure on producers to upgrade safety and quality. This pressure will also come from within India and regional export markets. First, with growing incomes and awareness, a growing segment of discerning consumers demands quality products. Second, growing access to regional markets and global value chains will bring into play the more stringent quality standards that international buyers use to coordinate their trade and satisfy distant customers. Third, regulators in India and other countries in the region are reforming food safety control by tightening legislation and improving the currently often lax and unsystematic enforcement. In the face of these changes, this chapter has sought to understand how product standards and related procedures constrain NER's trade with its neighbors, and how to ease such constraints.

More stringent food control, represented by evolving standards and related procedures, has the potential to create trade friction and develop into nontariff barriers. Policy makers and academics still debate the degree to which standards and related procedures cause trade friction in South Asia and contribute to low exports from NER. Standards diverge across borders in the region because they are developed without consultation between countries. But a significant, although unknown, portion of trade is informal. Traders frequently succeed in bypassing trade regulations, including food safety regulations. In South Asian countries like Bangladesh, the authorities do not strictly enforce food safety rules, partly due to capacity constraints. Thus, food safety and other food regulations remain unenforced to a large extent for both imports and in the domestic markets. The literature is scarce but provides a few examples of exporters citing the lack of testing facilities at the borders as a constraint on their exports (e.g., CUTS 2014). There are many other potential explanations for low exports, including poor quality.

Yet food safety authorities like FSSAI and BFSA have demonstrated an interest in tightening food control. FSSAI leads this trend. FSSAI is working to introduce such modern food safety practices as risk-based import controls and the use of third-party laboratories for testing, while seeking to end the traditional approach of 100 percent inspection and testing of end products. The challenges of strengthening food controls are many, and thus reform will be a long process, introducing changes gradually and unevenly throughout India's many states and across many different foods and business operators. But the direction is clear.

Future trade will depend on developing a regional model for food control that enables the authorities to tighten food control while allowing trade to flow seamlessly. FSSAI has initiated a process that uses international good-practice tools, such as mutual recognition agreements and equivalency in trade with neighboring countries. Simultaneously, the South Asian Association for Regional Cooperation is supporting the harmonization of technical requirements across South Asia. The successful implementation of such initiatives will support national and regional food control by allowing the use of risk-based border controls and saving resources. Economizing on enforcement resources is paramount for successful domestic food safety control because of the immensity of the task.

Policy makers should consider the following steps:

- *Value chain interventions are critical for upgrading product quality in NER.*

NER's products often suffer from quality problems that will be solved not by focusing on investments in standards and related procedures but by improving production and trading practices. The development of services such as standards, testing, and certification will have the greatest chances of success if they are integrated into broader value chain development projects that also address production and trading practices.

- *Investment in quality infrastructure should focus on clearly identified demand from regulators or the business community. The laboratory investment plan should ensure that investments in laboratory development are coordinated across agencies.*

Generic capacity building without identified demand should be avoided.

Investments in laboratory development should be coordinated across agencies, while also taking into account the private sector supply of such services. Several government authorities are already in the process of developing new food laboratories, such as those in Assam and Tripura. The proliferation of laboratories and duplication of testing capacity in a region with demand still evolving can undermine the sustainability of the investments.

The feasibility of laboratory services should be explored by developing a laboratory business plan for sustainable access to laboratory services. The quality and quantity of testing services will be maximized by developing sustainable services where they are needed most—often not at border posts—and by drawing on all sources, including private investments. Agencies like FSSAI should expand their network of notified laboratories to include all suitable laboratories, including NABL-accredited laboratories.

To aid countries in drawing up a laboratory investment plan, the World Bank has developed a guide on how to invest in food laboratories (World Bank 2009).

- *In developing standards and investing in testing services, attention needs to be given to emerging products for discerning consumers.*

Emerging products may need appropriate standards. For example, the Indian government may seek to influence the development of international grading standards to ensure that such standards capture the quality characteristics of bamboo from NER and other parts of the country.

Private food standards, including those developed by Indian market participants, increasingly influence competitiveness and market access. Such private initiatives often complement the efforts of government regulatory agencies. Such agencies will likely include private initiatives directly in future regulation. The government may influence the process of setting private standards, which are key to accessing global supply chains and support their implementation.

The development of laboratories should also focus on emerging products such as fresh and organic foods. Several private firms that were consulted during fieldwork in Assam expressed demand for food testing for commercial reasons, mainly targeting the Indian market. However, some of these firms expressed skepticism about whether government laboratories would be able to develop a business culture suitable for commercial testing.

- *International best practice suggests the use of trade facilitation tools such as harmonization, equivalence, and mutual recognition for import control. The authorities should rely as little as possible on the traditional model of 100 percent inspection and testing of imports. Investment in border post laboratories should be kept low.*

The choice of trade facilitation instruments is still a matter of debate. Some observers recommend strengthening border control through investment in laboratories at border posts. Currently, few border stations have quick access to laboratories and depend on distant laboratories, leading to long delays, or let food be imported without the required testing and inspection.

Investment in border post laboratories should be kept low. Border facilities could prove a double-edged sword, serving to facilitate or hamper trade, especially if they are not run properly but are used for rent-seeking purposes. The existing regulatory program at NER's borders is "fluid," as exemplified by food safety enforcement at the Agartala (India)–Akhaura (Bangladesh) land customs station

(LCS), where import control follows the formal FSSAI rules, but the testing capabilities of the local laboratory are insufficient. Imports from Bangladesh flow in despite limited testing and despite local laboratory testing capability being restricted to only a small number of parameters. This situation is likely common for many border posts. While the current operations can be justified by a desire to keep trade flowing, such a program is vulnerable to rent-seeking.

International best practice suggests refraining from establishing expensive infrastructure at the border when possible and instead allowing trade to flow through the use of equivalence and mutual recognition agreements, as prescribed in WTO's SPS and TBT Agreements. Although laboratory capacity will indeed need to be expanded, it would be difficult and costly to do it at the border. Exporters would likely find it much more useful if it were done closer to the site of production.

The authorities should rely as little as possible on the traditional model of 100 percent inspection and testing and should instead introduce trade facilitation instruments such as harmonization, equivalence, and mutual recognition. The authorities should introduce measures of policy coordination, such as consultations and joint training efforts, to reach common ground on how to develop food standards rather than continuing the current practice of developing divergent food standards, as documented by CUTS (2019). Policy coordination measures should be used to build the necessary trust that will eventually allow countries like India and Bangladesh to negotiate and conclude equivalence and mutual recognition agreements.

Indeed, India, represented by FSSAI, is currently experimenting with the introduction of practices such as equivalence and mutual recognition. Recently, following a meeting between the prime ministers of India and Bangladesh, India demonstrated its willingness to recognize testing services in Bangladesh for exports of a number of processed food products from Bangladesh to India. FSSAI also indicated a general willingness to use such recognition agreements to promote regional trade. If effective, such agreements would greatly facilitate trade without the need for heavy investment in border infrastructure and the associated risk of rent-seeking.

NOTES

1. For details, see Inbar, "The New ISO Standard Bringing Bamboo Structures to the World." October 23, 2018, https://www.inbar.int/iso19624/.
2. NABL is a signatory to regional and international bodies, such as the Asia Pacific Laboratory Accreditation Cooperation and the International Laboratory Accreditation Cooperation.
3. EIC's website explains its responsibilities in greater detail. See Export Inspection Council, Government of India, https://eicindia.gov.in/About-EIC/About-US/About-US.aspx.
4. FSSAI's website explains the activities of Food Safety on Wheels. "Food Safety on Wheels," Food Safety and Standards Authority of India, New Delhi, http://www.fssai.gov.in/home/food-testing/Food-Safety-on-Wheels.html.
5. See Government of Assam, "Industries and Commerce, Regional Food Testing Laboratory." https://aidcltd.assam.gov.in/information-services/detail/rftl-regional-food-testing-laboratory-0.
6. "Orders and Guidelines on Imports of Food Articles," Food Safety and Standards Authority of India, New Delhi, http://fssai.gov.in/home/imports/order-guidelines.html.
7. The full scale was 1 = very easy; 2 = easy; 3 = average; 4 = hard; 5 = very hard. The ranking does not distinguish between measures that are difficult to meet because they are unreasonable and those that are difficult to meet but regulate a legitimate issue. A barrier that received all 5s might not be judged illegitimate under WTO's SPS or TBT Agreements.

8. N. Bhaskar (adviser on quality assurance, Food Safety and Standards Authority of India), in discussion with World Bank staff, June 20, 2017.

9. See "Post Harvest Improvement Program for Other Spices," Spices Board India, Ministry of Commerce and Industry, Government of India, New Delhi, http://www.indianspices .com/post-harvest-improvement-programme.

10. See Khanna (2019) on fruit and vegetable value chains and the importance of end-to-end temperature controlled cold chains, extending from farm to market, to ensure that high-quality, fresh products can reach quality-conscious end consumers in distant markets.

REFERENCES

Basher, Mohammad Abul. 2013. *Indo-Bangla Trade: Composition, Trends and Way Forward.* London: Commonwealth Secretariat.

BFSA (Bangladesh Food Safety Authority). 2019. "Harmonization of Bangladesh's Food Safety Standards with Codex Standards and Other International Best Practices." BFSA, Dhaka. http://bfsa.gov.bd/index.php?option=com_content&view=article&layout=edit&id=280.

BSTI (Bangladesh Standards and Testing Institution). 2018. *BSTI Standards Catalogue 2018.* Dhaka: BSTI. https://bstibds.com/catalouge.

Chinzakhum. 2014. "Production and Marketing of Pineapple: A Study in Cachar District, Assam." Ph.D. thesis submitted to the Department of Commerce, Mahatma Gandhi School of Economics and Commerce, Assam University, Assam, India. http://shodhganga.inflibnet .ac.in/handle/10603/36521.

Clarke, Renata. 2010. "Private Food Safety Standards: Their Role in Food Safety Regulation and Their Impact." Paper presented at the 33rd Session of the Codex Alimentarius Commission, Food and Agriculture Organization of the United Nations, Rome, July 5–9.

CUTS (Consumer Utility and Trust Society). 2013. "Enhancing Trade and Regional Economic Integration between India and Bangladesh Phase I." CUTS International, Jaipur.

———. 2014. "India-Bangladesh Trade Potentiality: An Assessment of Trade Facilitation Issues." CUTS International, Jaipur.

———. 2019. "India-Bangladesh Agriculture Trade: Demystifying Non-Tariff Barriers to India-Bangladesh Trade in Agricultural Products and the Linkages with Food Security and Livelihood." CUTS International, Jaipur.

De, Prabir, and Manab Majumdar. 2014. *Developing Cross-Border Production Networks between North Eastern Region of India, Bangladesh and Myanmar.* New Delhi: Research and Information System for Developing Countries.

Dhar, Biswajit, Prabir De, Gurudas Das, and E. Bijoy Singh. 2011. *Expansion of North East India's Trade and Investment with Bangladesh and Myanmar: An Assessment of the Opportunities and Constraints.* New Delhi: Research and Information System for Developing Countries and the Ministry for the Development of the North Eastern Region, North Eastern Council, Government of India, New Delhi.

European Commission. 2009. "Commission Regulation (EC) No. 669/2009 of 24 July 2009 Implementing Regulation No. 882/2004 of the European Parliament and of the Council as Regards the Increased Level of Official Controls on Imports of Certain Feed and Food of Non-Animal Origin and Amending Decision 2006/504/EC." European Commission, Brussels.

———. 2014. "Commission Implementing Regulation (EU) No. 885/2014 of 13 August 2014 Laying Down Specific Conditions Applicable to the Import of Okra and Curry Leaves from India and Repealing Implementing Regulation (EU) No. 91/2013." European Commission, Brussels.

Fafchamps, Marcel, Ruth Vargas Hill, and Bart Minten. 2007. "Quality Control and the Marketing of Non-Staple Crops in India." In *Global Supply Chains, Standards, and the Poor,* edited by Johan Swinnen, 122–32. Wallingford, UK: Cabi Publications.

———. 2008. "Quality Control in Non-Staple Food Markets: Evidence from India." *Agricultural Economics* 38 (3): 251–66.

Fahrion, A. S., L. Jamir, K. Richa, S. Begum, V. Rutsa, S. Ao, V.P. Padmakumar, R.P. Deka, and D. Grace. 2014. "Food-Safety Hazards in the Pork Chain in Nagaland, North East India: Implications for Human Health." *International Journal of Environmental Research and Public Health* 11: 403–17.

FAO (Food and Agriculture Organization). 2016. *Risk Based Imported Food Control Manual.* Rome: FAO.

Grace, Delia. 2015. "Food Safety in Low and Middle Income Countries." *International Journal of Environmental Research and Public Health* 12: 10490–10507.

ILRI (International Livestock Research Institute). 2007. *Comprehensive Study of the Assam Dairy Sector: Action Plan for Pro-Poor Dairy Development.* Nairobi: ILRI.

Islam, Mohammad Monirul. 2011. "Trade Cooperation between Bangladesh and India with Special Reference to the North-East India." *Dialogue* 12 (4). http://www.asthabharati.org/Dia_Apr%20011/moh.htm.

Jaffee, Steven, Spencer Henson, and Luz Diaz Rios. 2011. "Making the Grade: Smallholder Farmers, Emerging Standards, and Development Assistance Programs in Africa—A Research Program Synthesis." Economic and Sector Work No. 2823, World Bank, Washington, DC.

Jensen, Michael Friis. 2016. "Meeting the Quality Challenge: Technical Regulation, Sanitary and Phytosanitary Measures, and Quality Infrastructure." In *Strengthening Competitiveness in Bangladesh: Thematic Assessment. A Diagnostic Trade Integration Study,* edited by Sanjay Kathuria and Mariem Mezghenni Malouche, 155–92. Washington, DC: World Bank.

Khanna, A. 2019. "Developing Inclusive Cross-Border Value Chains in North East India: Fruits and Vegetables." In *Strengthening Cross-Border Value Chains: Opportunities for India and Bangladesh,* ed. Sanjay Kathuria and Priya Mathur, chapter 2. World Bank, Washington, DC.

Lapar, L., R. Deka, J. Lindahl, and D. Grace. 2014. *Quality and Safety Improvements in Informal Milk Markets and Implications for Food Safety Policy.* Nairobi: International Livestock Research Institute.

Manghnani, R. 2019. "Developing Inclusive Cross-Border Value Chains in North East India: Bamboo and Bamboo Products." In *Strengthening Cross-Border Value Chains: Opportunities for India and Bangladesh,* ed. Sanjay Kathuria and Priya Mathur, chapter 3. World Bank, Washington, DC.

NABL (National Accreditation Board for Testing and Calibration Laboratories). 2018. "Laboratory Search." NABL, Ministry of Commerce and Industry, Government of India (accessed July 4, 2018), https://www.nabl-india.org/nabl/index.php?c=search&m=index&Itemid=177.

New Age. 2017. "Food Safety Big Challenge for Bangladesh." August 19, http://www.newagebd.net/article/22352/food-safety-big-challenge-for-bdesh.

Rahman, Mustafizur, Mazbahul Golam Ahamad, A.K.M. Nazrul Islam, and Muhammad Al Amin. 2012. "Agricultural Trade between Bangladesh and India: An Analysis of Trends, Trading Patterns and Determinants." CPD-CMI Working Paper 3, Centre for Policy Dialogue, Dhaka, and Chr. Michelsen Institute, Bergen, Norway.

Spices Board of India. Undated. "Mandatory Tests Required for Export of Spices and Spice Products." Spices Board of India, Kochi, India (accessed November 7, 2017), http://indianspices.com/sites/default/files/Mandatory%20tests%20required%20for%20export%20of%20Spices%20and%20Spice%20%20%20products%202017%20new.pdf.

Taneja, Nisha. 2018. "A Granular Approach to Addressing Nontariff Barriers: India's Trade with Bangladesh and Nepal." In *A Glass Half Full: The Promise of Regional Trade in South Asia,* edited by Sanjay Kathuria, 105–58. Washington, DC: World Bank.

Trujillo, David, and Suneina Jangra. 2016. "Grading of Bamboo." INBAR Working Paper 79, International Network for Bamboo & Rattan and Coventry University, Coventry, United Kingdom.

USDA (United States Department of Agriculture). 2016. "Exporter's Guide Bangladesh 2016." GAIN Report Number 6007, USDA Foreign Agricultural Service, Global Agricultural Information Network, USDA, Washington, DC.

WHO (World Health Organization). 2015. *WHO Estimates of the Global Burden of Foodborne Diseases.* Foodborne Diseases Burden Epidemiology Reference Group 2007–2015. Geneva: WHO.

World Bank. 2009. *Guide for Assessing Investment Needs in Laboratory Capacities for Managing Food Safety, Plant Health, and Animal Health.* Washington, DC: World Bank.

Yang, Hanzhou. 2017. "Food Safety in India: Status and Challenges." TCI-TARINA Policy Brief No. 5, Tata-Cornell Institute for Agriculture and Nutrition–Technical Assistance and Research for Indian Nutrition and Agriculture, Ithaca, NY.